MIRACLES STILL HAPPEN

· · ·

RICHARD LEE

WORD PUBLISHING
Dallas · London · Sydney · Singapore

MIRACLES STILL HAPPEN: DISCOVERING GOD'S POWER IN
YOUR LIFE

Unless otherwise indicated, Scripture quotations used in this book are
from The King James Version of the Bible.

Other Bible versions used include:

The Living Bible (TLB), copyright 1971 by Tyndale House Publish-
ers, Wheaton, IL. Used by permission.
The New King James Version (NKJV). Copyright © 1979, 1980,
1982, Thomas Nelson, Inc., Publisher.

An effort has been made to locate sources and obtain permission
where necessary for the quotations used in this book. In the event of
any unintentional omission, modifications will be gladly incorporated
in future editions.

Library of Congress Cataloging-in-Publication Data:

Lee, Richard, 1946–
    Miracles still happen : discovering God's power in your life
    Richard Lee.
        p.   cm.
    ISBN 0–8499–0666–0
    1. Christian life—1960–   2. Miracles.   I. Title
    BV4501.2.L4253   1989
    231.7′3—dc20   89–9006
                                                     CIP

Printed in the United States of America

9 8 0 1 2 3 9 RRD 9 8 7 6 5 4 3 2 1

Affectionately dedicated to

JUDITH STARR LEE

My loving wife, best friend,
and special gift from God.

CONTENTS

INTRODUCTION

Do miracles still happen? Certainly they do! By definition, a miracle is a supernatural work of God which contradicts the laws of nature. The meaning of the Hebrew word for *miracle* is "to be different." Therefore, a miracle is that which is remarkable or unique. It is a supernatural phenomenon that only God can produce. It is not a mere coincidence of circumstances.

Miracles are divine interruptions into the normal course of history, those distinctive events which defy the laws of nature. The Bible is filled with such accounts in relation to the ministry of the Old Testament prophets, and to the ministry of Jesus Christ and the apostles in the New Testament. Some of these miracles were aimed at nature; others, the physical healing of those who were sick; still others were aimed at meeting the needs of those in troubled situations. But the *real* miracle of every miracle in the Bible is the greater one that God works in the hearts of men and women, boys and girls. That's the truly lasting miracle. While physical miracles pass away, those that happen in our hearts last for eternity—and they are just as supernatural in nature because they also defy the laws of the natural man.

That's why I have written this book—to look at the miracles of the Bible in a refreshingly new way . . . to reveal the miracle within each miracle that so many have overlooked for so long . . . to share with you the good news that these same life-changing miracles can and will happen in our lives today. As one writer once put it:

A hundred million miracles
Are happening every day.
But only those who have the faith
Can see them on life's way.

I want to express my appreciation to those who have helped and encouraged me in the writing of this book: the wonderful people of Rehoboth Baptist Church who so willingly share their pastor's ministry with others; Dr. Jim Black and Beverly Phillips at Word Publishing for their guidance along the way; my friend Dr. Ed Hindson for his valued advice; and, of course, my devoted secretary, Emily Boothe, who took her pastor's scribbled notes and made sense of it all.

Now may God direct and bless you on this exciting journey as you seek His miracle for your life.

Richard G. Lee

1

WHEN YOU REACH THE BOTTOM OF THE BARREL

■   ■   ■

The Miracle of Trust

1 Kings 17:8–16

8   And the word of the Lord came unto him, saying,

9   Arise, get thee to Zarephath, which belongeth to Zidon, and dwell there: behold, I have commanded a widow woman there to sustain thee.

10   So he arose and went to Zarephath. And when he came to the gate of the city, behold, the widow woman was there gathering of sticks: and he called to her, and said, Fetch me, I pray thee, a little water in a vessel, that I may drink.

11   And as she was going to fetch it, he called to her, and said, Bring me, I pray thee, a morsel of bread in thine hand.

12   And she said, As the Lord thy God liveth, I have not a cake, but a handful of meal in a barrel, and a little oil in a cruse: and, behold, I am gathering two sticks, that I may go in and dress it for me and my son, that we may eat it, and die.

13   And Elijah said unto her, Fear not; go and do as thou hast said: but make me thereof a little cake first, and bring it unto me, and after make for thee and for thy son.

14   For thus saith the Lord God of Israel, The barrel of meal shall not waste, neither shall the cruse of oil fail, until the day that the Lord sendeth rain upon the earth.

15   And she went and did according to the saying of Elijah: and she, and he, and her house, did eat many days.

16   And the barrel of meal wasted not, neither did the cruse of oil fail, according to the word of the Lord, which he spake unto Elijah.

There is a story about a fellow who was hiking through the mountains one day when he fell off a cliff and plunged a hundred feet before he was able to catch hold of a limb that was jutting out of the mountainside. Looking down, he could see the rocks a thousand feet below. Above him was the sheer face of the cliff with no visible means for climbing to the top. Seeing his plight, he cried, "Help me! Somebody help me! Is anybody up there?" Suddenly, a voice came back, *"I am God, and I am here to help you. Trust me and just let go of the limb—trust Me."* The man looked down a thousand feet, then looked up again and shouted, "Is anybody *else* up there?"

There have been times when I seemed to be holding on to some twig of life, when one slip would bring certain disaster. Almost inevitably, however, God would say to me, "Richard, now let go and trust me." I have to admit that at times like this I, too, have wanted to know if there was anybody else up there.

It isn't easy to simply let go and trust God. But that is the very essence of real faith: letting go of that in which we find our security outside of God.

In 1 Kings 17, we are given a classic example of what can happen when we release the limb of our own security and trust in God. The story is that of a widow whose name we do not know—the Bible calls her simply the widow of Zarephath. But her trust in God has become legendary.

During the time of this story, the land of Zarephath was experiencing a great drought. It hadn't rained for months. The rivers were drying up, and the crops were failing. Because of the lack of food, many were dying of starvation, and this widow and her small son were no exception.

On this particular day, she found herself with only a little meal left in her barrel and a small portion of cooking oil in her cruse—just enough for one last meal for her and her son. She had resigned herself to the fact that when this was gone, she and her son would die. What a terrible fate, what a horrible ending—starving to death. It would seem to be the end of her story, but, in fact, it was only the beginning. God had a different plan.

Into the scene steps God's prophet, Elijah, and as we listen in, God speaks to His prophet, sending him to the widow:

And the word of the Lord came unto him, saying Arise, get thee to Zarephath, which belongeth to Zidon, and dwell there: behold, I have commanded a widow woman there to sustain thee. (vv. 8–9)

What strikes me most about this passage is not that God was sending His prophet, Elijah, to be with the widow, but that the words *behold, I have commanded a widow woman to sustain thee* indicate that God had already been there. God had visited the scene *before* the widow's problem ever came to be. That has within it a great spiritual truth: *When our need is greatest—God is nearest.*

WHEN OUR NEED IS GREATEST— GOD IS NEAREST

We will never have a problem that takes God by surprise. Whatever our mountain of impossibility or valley of despair, God has already surveyed it and is waiting to guide us through it. As the great Master Planner of our lives, He has already chosen the path before us. That is why the wonderful truth in Romans 8:28 is so dear to us. In this passage, God's reminder of comfort and assurance is that "all things work together for good to them that love God, to them who are the called according to his purpose."

How can we be certain that all things will work together for good? Because where we are headed, walking in His will, God has gone before and made a clear path for our journey.

The Psalmist wrote, "The steps of a good man are ordered by the Lord, and he delighteth in his way" (37:23). I especially like the word *ordered*. It comes from the Hebrew word *kuwn*, meaning "prepared." One modern translator says the verse carries the connotation of bulldozing one's way through a situation. But it also says God delights in each step of life that we take. You may ask, "How could He? How could God delight in watching me go through my trials and testings? When life doesn't seem to fit together and my way is uncertain, how can God delight in that?"

The answer lies in the story of the little boy whose father bought him a picture puzzle for Christmas. All one afternoon, the little boy tried without success to put the puzzle together. He even tried forcing the pieces to interlock, but they would not fit. Finally, handing the puzzle to his father, he said, "Here, Dad,

you give it a try. I quit. I could never put it together."
After a few minutes the father completed the puzzle.
"How did you do that?" the boy asked. "It wasn't so
hard," said his father. "You see, I've seen the whole
picture of the puzzle, while you've only seen the
pieces."

In the same way, God sees the whole picture of our
lives. Like the little boy, we see only the pieces and
become impatient trying to make them fit, trying to
force one situation after another into place. If we
would simply yield ourselves into the hands of God and
trust Him fully, He who has seen the whole picture
could put the puzzle of our lives together perfectly.

OUR LAST SUPPLY BECOMES GOD'S
FIRST CONCERN

Humanly speaking, the widow of Zarephath had
reached the "bottom of her barrel." She said in verse
12, "As the Lord thy God liveth, I have not a cake, but
a handful of meal in a barrel, and a little oil in a cruse:
and, behold, I am gathering two sticks, that I may go in
and dress it for me and my son, that we may eat it, and
die." Here we find the real story. It is not one of feeding the prophet, for God could have fed Elijah in many
ways. (In fact, earlier in the chapter He had sent ravens
to feed him.) The real story is centered upon the fact
that the widow had reached the end of her earthly
supply. She had no one but God to save her, and that is
when God comes to her rescue—when her human resources were depleted and trusting God was her only
hope. And, oh, what hope she found in Him. Annie
Johnson Flint said it in her hymn, *He Giveth More Grace:*

When we have exhausted our store of endurance,
When our strength has failed ere the day is half done,
When we reach the end of our hoarded resources,
Our Father's full giving is only begun.

His love has no limit, His grace has no measure,
His power has no boundary known unto men:
For out of His infinite riches in Jesus,
He giveth, and giveth, and giveth again!

When we reach the end of our self-sufficiency and find ourselves at the bottom of the barrel of life, we, too, can have the reassurance that God is still there. He is lovingly and tenderly reaching out to us to meet us at the point of our greatest need. In essence, the Lord is reminding us that when all else has failed, we can always trust in Him.

One of the reasons that many of us never receive the help which God makes available to us is that we have learned to depend on too many resources outside of Him. We are so quick to turn to the material and social solutions of our own time that we can forget that what we really need is the grace and help of God to meet our needs. It is difficult for modern men and women to really put their faith and confidence in God when there are so many other things on which to rely. "Why should I be in a hurry to get to Heaven?" someone once asked me. "I have a new house, swimming pool, and a brand new car!" It wasn't that he didn't want to go to Heaven eventually, he just didn't want to go right now! When we have so many things clamoring for our attention, it is hard for us to focus on that which is spiritual and eternal. It is not that we do not want God in our lives, but as long as things are basically going well for us, we tend to treat Him as some sort of extra added attraction.

It is unfortunate that we frequently have to reach the end of our human and worldly resources in order to really appreciate who God is and what He can do for us. Too often, it is only when we are forced by the circumstances of life to focus our attention on Him that we can really begin to appreciate all that He is and all that He can do for us.

GOD ASKS MUCH WHEN HE WANTS TO GIVE MUCH

When the widow told the prophet Elijah of her plight, he did the very opposite of what most of us would have expected him to do. Instead of revealing to her that he was sent by God to meet her needs, he told her to make him something to eat first and then to feed herself and her son with what was left over. A casual reading of this passage might leave one with the impression that the prophet was insensitive and selfish. He asked for the greatest possession in the widow's life. In fact, since she was facing the possibility of death, his request was equivalent to asking for her life itself.

You may find that shocking. But it's really no different from what God asks of us today. He will always demand that we surrender unto Him the greatest possession of our lives. But why? Is God trying to rob us of our joy? Is He trying to take away those things that make us happy? Not at all. I didn't say that God would take our greatest possession away, only that He would demand its *surrender* unto Him. Remember the first commandment, "I am the Lord thy God . . . thou shalt have no other gods before me." He wants nothing in our lives to be greater than He is—nothing we trust more than we do Him. God is telling us that if He is going to give His all to us, we must be willing to give our all to Him. How can we do less?

When this widow gave all that she had, she was acknowledging that God had first priority in her life. Her act of kindness was also an act of trust and obedience. While God was about to provide miraculously for her physical needs, He was also developing a spiritual miracle in the depth of her soul. We cannot totally respond to God in sacrificial giving of ourselves until we have learned to place our absolute trust and confidence in Him.

The more we trust the Lord with the details *of* our lives, the more we will see His blessing *in* our lives. It is not that God withholds good from us and only gives it to us when we deserve it. Rather, the principle of Scripture is that God delights to bless us when we trust Him for our deepest needs. For it is then, and perhaps only then, that our attention is so focused upon Him that we realize that He alone is the source of fulfillment for all our needs.

WHEN WE GIVE IN FAITH, GOD BLESSES IN ABUNDANCE

The story of Elijah and the widow has a very beautiful ending. Once she had fed the prophet by faith and put her confidence in God, the Scripture says, "And the barrel of meal wasted not, neither did the cruse of oil fail, according to the word of the Lord, which he spake unto Elijah" (1 Kings 17:16). Notice that God not only kept His promise, but He did so in abundance. He met every need that the widow and her son had.

I remember reading a story once about an elderly woman who was praying for a bag of flour during the days of the Great Depression. It was her custom to pray on her front porch for her daily needs. One day as she was praying and asking God to send her a bag of flour, two boys were passing by and overheard her prayer. Thinking they would play a joke on her, the boys went to the corner grocery store and bought two bags of flour and brought them back to the woman's house. They climbed up the back of the house and slid the two bags down the tin roof onto the porch. When she saw the bags of flour, she began to shout, "Oh, thank you, God, thank you for sending me this flour." At that moment, the two boys came around the house and said, "Old woman, God didn't send you that flour—we did!" The woman turned to the two boys and said, "Boys, God did send the flour to me, even if He had to use you two little devils to bring it!"

We may not always be able to determine *how* God will answer our prayers and meet our needs, but we can have the confidence that *He will.*

Just as the widow of Zarephath trusted God when she reached the bottom of her barrel, so you and I must learn the miracle of trust in our own lives. Faith is not something that we exercise merely by human effort or self-discipline. The Bible makes it clear that faith is a fruit of the Spirit and a gift from God. As God works in our hearts to produce the miracle of trust, He is reminding us that He is there and His power is at work on our behalf.

Perhaps you have come to the bottom of your barrel—life looks bleak, difficult, even impossible, and you are tired of being disappointed by the promises of others. If you are looking for someone to trust today, let me recommend the God of Scripture who will never fail you nor disappoint you. The greatest miracle that can take place in our lives is not that our needs are met, but that our hearts learn to trust the God who alone can meet those needs.

You do not have to face the pressures and problems of life alone. An all-wise and all-loving God will always provide exactly what you need, when you need it. All you have to do is trust Him to meet those needs. Once you do, your miracle has already begun!

2

MAKING YOUR DREAMS COME TRUE

■   ■   ■

The Miracle of Surrender

John 6:5–14

5   When Jesus then lifted up his eyes, and saw a great company come unto him, he saith unto Philip, Whence shall we buy bread, that these may eat?

6   And this he said to prove him: for he himself knew what he would do.

7   Philip answered him, Two hundred pennyworth of bread is not sufficient for them, that every one of them may take a little.

8   One of his disciples, Andrew, Simon Peter's brother, saith unto him,

9   There is a lad here, which hath five barley loaves, and two small fishes: but what are they among so many?

10   And Jesus said, Make the men sit down. Now there was much grass in the place. So the men sat down, in number about five thousand.

11   And Jesus took the loaves; and when he had given thanks, he distributed to the disciples, and the disciples to them that were set down; and likewise of the fishes as much as they would.

12   When they were filled, he said unto his disciples, Gather up the fragments that remain, that nothing be lost.

13   Therefore they gathered them together, and filled twelve baskets with the fragments of the five barley loaves, which remained over and above unto them that had eaten.

14   Then those men, when they had seen the miracle that Jesus did, said, This is of a truth that Prophet that should come into the world.

I think we all want to count in life. We want to make a difference some how, some way, in our world.

The little girl shuts herself in her room and dances with dreams of one day being a ballerina. The freckled-faced boy bounces the ball off the side of the house, catching it in his glove and dreaming of the Big Leagues. The student dreams of his diploma; the graduate, that promising new job; the worker, that long-sought-after promotion. What do all these have in common? They are dreaming that they will count for something, that one day they will "make it in life," and that because of them, things will be different. I have good news for everyone who has dreamed such dreams: God created every person to make a difference in this world. There is no one who doesn't really count. No one is a nonessential part of His plan.

In this chapter, I want to point you toward *surrender*. The miracle of surrender is the key that places your dreams and aspirations into the hands of our eternal God, who is able to cause all our dreams to come true and our lives to reach their fullest potential.

There is no greater story in the Bible to illustrate this than the miracle found in John 6:5–14. Here Jesus and His disciples were faced with a challenging situation. As Christ had begun teaching upon a mountain side, a great multitude had gathered to hear Him. The

15

Bible says there were about five thousand men in the crowd that day. When these people became hungry, the disciples were perplexed at how they would feed them all. Certainly they didn't have the food to feed them. What would they do?

At that very moment, Andrew, one of the disciples, announced that there was a small boy in the crowd who had five barley loaves and two fishes, adding, "But what are they among so many?" The Lord took the food which the boy had surrendered to Him, blessed the loaves, and gave them to the disciples to distribute to the people. Then He did the same thing with the fish. As the disciples moved from person to person handing out bread, there continued to be an endless supply left in their hands and likewise with the fish. In fact, the Bible tells us that when they were finished, they had not only fed the entire multitude but they also collected twelve baskets full of leftover fragments!

Imagine, one small boy, through a simple act of surrender, became the central figure in one of the most phenomenal miracles that Jesus ever performed. His one act of surrender made a difference for thousands of people. In the same way, you and I can never underestimate the significance of a single act of surrender on our part in our own day and age; we, too, can be part of God's miracle in our world.

Perhaps you are just living from day to day. Perhaps there doesn't seem to be any special significance about your life at all. You simply get up in the morning, go to work for the day, and go to bed at night. Your life is caught in the routines of life and doesn't seem to have any real purpose.

Perhaps you feel a little like the man in the following poem:

Poor, poor, Solomon Grundy,
Born on Monday,
Christened on Tuesday,
Married on Wednesday,
Sick on Thursday,
Sicker on Friday,
Died on Saturday,
Buried on Sunday,
And that was the end of Solomon Grundy.

It may be that in the daily grind you feel that life isn't worth living after all. You may have once dreamed great dreams, but now you feel your dreams have died. Well, if that is the case, I've good news for you. You can dream again! And you can see your dreams come true as you learn the secret of surrendering your life to the God who makes dreams come true. In the story of this one little boy who was a vital part of Jesus' miracle, we find principles that can make dreams happen.

THE RIGHT PLACE AT THE RIGHT TIME

Notice first of all that the little boy was in the right place at the right time. Just when the disciples were most desperate to decide what to do about the needs of the multitude, this boy appeared with his lunch. We are not told who he was, where he came from, or how he got there. He may well have come with his parents, or perhaps he had left home that morning with a lunch packed by a thoughtful mother and had made his way to the edge of town to hear this wonderful Teacher. Whatever the case may have been, the boy was in exactly the right place to offer his simple act of surrender which touched the lives of thousands of people that day.

Finding success in the will of God also depends upon being in the right place at the right time. I have often heard businessmen comment on the success of someone else by saying, "Oh, he was just lucky to be in the right place at the right time." But I have found that, more often than not, successful people are in the right place at the right time because they have already made certain important decisions that placed them there. For example, the little boy we just read about was in the right place at the right time because someone, either he or his mother, had taken time to prepare his lunch. Proper preparation will always pay off. This is true in every area of our lives. In business or vocation, we may eventually benefit from years of preparation, organization, and planning. In other instances, a limited amount of preparation may bring immediate benefits. Whatever the case may be, the point is that things just don't happen by accident.

In the Christian life, there are specific things that we can know for certain. First of all, I can be certain that I am in a right relationship with God. The Bible tells us that Jesus Christ died for our sins so that He might reconcile us to God. It is possible for each of us to know beyond a shadow of a doubt that our sins have been forgiven and that our lives have been committed to Christ. That is the first step in being in the right place at the right time as far as God is concerned. Second, we can also know for certain that we are in the center of God's will when we are doing the things that He commands us to do. As much as some people struggle to find the will of God for their life, I have always been convinced that the will of God is not hard to find. God has written a manual for us which explains the steps to knowing His will and following it in every detail of our lives. That manual is the Bible. In it, God reveals His plan and purpose for our lives.

In Bible times, the concept of a "will" was similar to what we would call a last will and testament today. It was a specific statement of one's intended purposes, especially between a father and a son. The will of the father stated his relationship to his son as his heir and explained all that the father intended to give to his son. In the same way, the Bible is the specific statement of God's will and testament for the believer.

My son, Jason, now stands over 6'3", and although in my heart he still is my little boy, in reality he is now a young man. Suppose I were to say to him, "Jason, there is something that I want you to do for me. In fact, if you don't do it, you are going to get in trouble. But if you are willing to do it, I'm going to give you a great reward."

Let's assume that he indicates that he is willing to do what I ask. Then, after I remind him that his response will either bring him great joy or great trouble, he asks, "Dad, what is it you want me to do?"

I respond, "I am not going to tell you! I am simply going to let you guess what I want you to do."

Obviously, this is an utterly foolish scenario. No father would rightfully ask his son to do something without explaining what it was he wanted him to do. In fact, if the father were convinced that this would benefit his son, he would tell him very clearly and explicitly what to do. He might even write it down for him so he would not forget it. That is exactly what God, our heavenly Father, has done for us. He has taken the time to write His will for us in black and white in the pages of Scripture.

Let me share with you *six ways* that I have found to be effective in discovering God's will in my own life. These have aided me in being in the right place with God.

The first source of knowing God's will is *the Word of God.* The Psalmist said, "Thy word is a lamp unto my feet, and a light unto my path" (Psalm 119:105). God has detailed His plan in the Bible. To ignore it is to disregard the greatest source of knowing God's will, but to study it carefully and follow it completely is the wisest thing we can do.

The second way to discover God's will is *the witness of the Holy Spirit.* Jesus promised us, "Howbeit when he, the Spirit of truth, is come, he will guide you into all truth: for he shall not speak of himself; but whatsoever he shall hear, that shall he speak: and he will shew you things to come" (John 16:13). God has placed within all of His children the presence of the Holy Spirit to guide us. But we must give Him a chance to speak to our hearts through prayer and meditation upon His Word.

The third way for finding God's will is *the walk of fellowship.* This is the knowledge that comes from our daily walk with God. In the Old Testament we are told that "Enoch walked with God" (Genesis 5:24). We, too, can walk with God each day. The longer we walk with Him in fellowship, the greater our ability to understand His perfect will.

A few months ago, as I was preparing for the funeral service of one of the men in our church, I met with the man's widow and children and asked if they knew of any particular thing that he might like to have done at his funeral. Instantly his wife replied with a certain request. "I know he would have wanted it," she said. One of the daughters looked at her and asked how she could be so certain her father would have wanted it that way. The mother replied, "Honey, I lived with your father for forty-eight years. After that long, I think I would know what he wanted."

The same applies to our walk of fellowship with God. The longer we walk with Him in sweet and close fellowship, the more apt we are to understand His will when we face life's decisions.

The fourth way to know God's will is *the wisdom that God giveth.* The apostle James tells us that God will give wisdom liberally to those who ask for it in prayer (James 1:5). It is reassuring to know that God is ready and willing to give us wisdom if we are willing to ask for it and put ourselves in the relationship with Him in which we can receive it.

The fifth source for knowing God's will is *the workers of God.* These are our fellow believers who have themselves been through many of the trials and testings that face us and are willing to give us Godly counsel concerning direction for our lives.

The sixth means I have found for knowing God's will is *the works of God.* There is a beautiful promise in Psalm 32:8. It says, "I will instruct thee and teach thee in the way which thou shalt go: I will guide thee with mine eye." Part of His guiding process is the opening and closing of doors of opportunity before us. This is often the clearest way of discerning His will. But when God closes a door, we must be careful not to ignore His will by trying to force our way in. As a man many years my senior once told me, "Son, if you've prayed about a matter and God has shut the door, don't go around back and try to crawl through the window!"

Never forget that God is a loving heavenly Father. All of the generosity and kindness that a loving earthly father would extend to his family, God gives to us and a thousand times more. He does not leave the understanding of His will to conjecture. Rather, He has stated clearly what He wants us to do. It is up to us to put ourselves in the right place, for it is there that we can be used by God.

GO WITH WHAT YOU ALREADY HAVE

The success of the little boy's involvement in the miracle which Jesus performed is in the fact that he was willing to offer what little that he had. All too often, people fail to respond to God by faith because they believe that what they have to offer Him is so insignificant that God could not use it. When Andrew brought the boy to Jesus with the barley loaves and the fishes, he said, "But what are they among so many?" While Andrew should be commended for at least bringing the boy and his lunch to Jesus, he still expressed his own doubt as to the significance of such an offer.

Like so many of us, Andrew temporarily forgot that he was speaking to the Creator Himself. This was not some simple rabbi who could do little more than divide it among a handful of people. This was the very One who could bless and multiply the offering so that it would adequately feed a great multitude of people. How many times do we feel that what we have to offer God is so small and insignificant that it will make very little difference?

When we focus on our inabilities and fail to focus on His ability, we can feel that our service to God is worthless. In a very real sense, we *are* worthless, in and of ourselves. But when we offer even our most inadequate service to God, He has promised to bless and multiply it beyond our wildest expectations. Think of all of the people in the Bible that God used in spite of their shortcomings. Gideon was a coward who was afraid of his own shadow, yet God turned him into a mighty warrior and leader of Israel. Isaiah, the prophet, said that he was unclean and unfit for the ministry, yet God used him to write one of the greatest books of the Old Testament. The apostle Paul called himself the "chief of sinners," and despite his early resistance to the message of the gospel, he became the greatest gospel preacher who ever lived. The apostle Peter bitterly denied the Lord the night before His crucifixion, but he later preached one of the greatest sermons ever given. David was just a teenager when he stood before the mighty Goliath, yet when the opportunity presented itself for him to stand against the great Philistine warrior, he went forth without armor, taking with him only a small sling he used every day and five stones.

God is not looking for people who want to make a difference by their own effort. Rather, He is looking for those who are willing to go and serve Him with what abilities or inabilities they already have. You do not have to become great in order to do great things for God. Just offer yourself to Him and follow the dream He has placed in your heart. Stop waiting for God to put something you consider "special" into your hand before you offer Him that which is already there. The little boy with the five loaves and two fish could have easily said to himself that his lunch was too small or not good enough to be used by Jesus and merely kept it hidden. Or he could have wasted time trying to collect more food from other sources. However, he did what any one of us can do—he offered the Savior what he already had.

GIVE GOD ALL THAT YOU HAVE

We are not told what thoughts must have gone through the mind of this boy as he offered his lunch to Andrew and Andrew in turn offered it to Jesus. If he had been like many Christians today, he would have eaten half of the lunch and offered the other half to the Savior. Unfortunately, that is how many of us operate today. We will give God Sunday morning, but we won't give Him Sunday night. We will think about what we ought to put into the offering plate and then give about half that amount! The wonderful thing about this lad is that he offered his entire lunch—all he had. Likewise, we must be willing to give to God and hold back nothing; only then will we experience His power at work in our lives. Just as the lad gave Jesus all that he had and the Savior blessed it and multiplied it, so will He do for you and me.

God deserves our very best. In light of all that He has done for us, He deserves our all. The Bible reminds us that God so loved the world that He gave us His Son; He gave us all that He had to give. How can we do less than give Him our very best as an act of surrender and service to Him? How can we hold back anything from God when He has given His only begotten Son for us?

Mr. or Ms. Businessperson, the greatest possession that you have is not your money or your job. It is the eternal relationship which you have with a living God. Money may come and go but Christ alone is everlasting. Mr. or Ms. Educator, you may have knowledge and wisdom, but remember, within the next ten years or so, much of your knowledge will become outdated. In God, however, you have the wisdom that surpasses all the understanding of this world. Mrs. Housewife, you may have a well-ordered life with all the security that this world can provide, but your greatest security is in your relationship to God and not in the things of this world. Young people, you have the joy and happiness of youth, but you will find that real joy and lasting peace come only from God and not from material possessions.

Imagine the wonderful joy and contentment that the little boy felt when he gave his entire lunch to Jesus Christ. Once he experienced the miracle in his heart, it resulted in the miracle of the feeding of the five thousand. There is no way that he could have ever imagined what would come from his simple offering. Likewise, you and I cannot imagine what will come from our lives being surrendered to the will and purpose of God.

WHAT A DIFFERENCE YOU CAN MAKE!

Once our Lord touched the simple offering of the young boy, he multiplied it so dramatically that it not only fed the thousands of people gathered on that hillside, but the Bible also tells us that the disciples collected twelve basketfuls of fragments over and above that which had been eaten! It was the touch of the Master's hand that changed everything that day. And that is the way that it still is today. One of the most wonderful things in a pastor's life is observing people when they genuinely come to God by faith and surrender what they have to His service. When they give their all, suddenly something wonderful and incredible begins to happen. Inevitably, they become amazed by what God is doing in their lives. I have often heard people say, "Pastor, you just can't believe what is happening in my business (or "in our home," or "in my life"). I never dreamed it could be so good."

What brings about such wonderful transformations? The principle is the same today as it was when Jesus was on earth. Surrender what you have totally and completely to God's service, and when you do, He will multiply it and use it to His glory!

The story of the feeding of the five thousand ends with the statement, "Then those men, when they had seen the miracle that Jesus did, said, This is of a truth the Prophet that should come into the world" (John 6:14). The miracle was so convincing that the crowd who had gathered to hear Jesus realized that He was no mere teacher or rabbi, but that He was the Prophet of God who Scripture predicted would come and turn the hearts of the people of Israel back to God.

God wants to do the very same kind of work in our lives today. If we are willing to surrender our all to Him and let Him use us to make a difference in our world, the end result will be that people will be attracted to our Savior. When others see what He can do with our lives, how He has helped our dreams come true, they will look beyond us to the One who has made all the difference.

> *I've dreamed many dreams that never came true*
> *I've seen them vanish at dawn,*
> *But I've realized enough of my dreams, thank God,*
> *To make me want to dream on.*

3

WALKING ON WATER

■ ■ ■

The Miracle of Confidence

Matthew 14:22–33

22   And straightway Jesus constrained his disciples to get into a ship, and to go before him unto the other side, while he sent the multitudes away.

23   And when he had sent the multitudes away, he went up into a mountain apart to pray: and when the evening was come, he was there alone.

24   But the ship was now in the midst of the sea, tossed with waves: for the wind was contrary.

25   And in the fourth watch of the night Jesus went unto them, walking on the sea.

26   And when the disciples saw him walking on the sea, they were troubled, saying, It is a spirit; and they cried out for fear.

27   But straightway Jesus spake unto them, saying, Be of good cheer; it is I; be not afraid.

28   And Peter answered him and said, Lord, if it be thou, bid me come unto thee on the water.

29   And he said, Come. And when Peter was come down out of the ship, he walked on the water, to go to Jesus.

30   But when he saw the wind boisterous, he was afraid; and beginning to sink, he cried, saying, Lord, save me.

31   And immediately Jesus stretched forth his hand, and caught him, and said unto him, O thou of little faith, wherefore didst thou doubt?

32   And when they were come into the ship, the wind ceased.

33   Then they that were in the ship came and worshipped him, saying, Of a truth thou art the Son of God.

What did you expect me to do?" Bill thundered at Joyce. "Walk on water?"

They had been having family conflicts for years and never seemed to be able to resolve them. Every discussion led to an argument and every attempt at a solution only seemed to increase their frustration. As the three of us talked together about finding God's help for their problems, I looked directly at Bill and said, "Yes, Bill, you *can* walk on water!"

"What do you mean?" he asked.

"If walking on water means doing the impossible," I suggested, "then I believe that you can do just that. You may not think that you can make the changes that are necessary to save your marriage, but I believe that God can help you make those changes. If you will trust Him, He will help you do the impossible."

"Can I really count on that?" Bill asked. "Yes!" I said emphatically. "God is still in the business of working miracles today!"

"You mean that miracles still happen today?" Joyce asked.

"Certainly I do," I replied, and as time passed, we began working on resolving problems in their marriage. While many of them were typical problems most modern couples face, some of them were extremely complicated and difficult. As we tackled these, I was

31

reminded again how sin always complicates our lives. However, God is still in the business of dealing with sin, resolving our difficulties, and uncomplicating our lives. It took a great deal of time to work through some of their problems, but eventually Bill and Joyce came to the realization that no matter how difficult their circumstances seemed to be, God's power was even greater still.

When most of us face seemingly insurmountable obstacles in our lives, we tend to want to run away from them. At the very time when we need to act responsibly, we tend to become most irresponsible. But running away solves nothing. There comes a time when we must face our challenges head-on and take responsibility for our actions. At the same time, there will always come a point at which we must be willing to allow our faith and trust in God to help us meet those problems.

One of the most powerful accounts of miracle-working trust is found in Matthew 14:22–33 in the story of Peter walking on the water. The disciples had left Jesus on the shore and set out in a boat to cross the Sea of Galilee. A storm suddenly rose up against them and they found themselves struggling for their very lives. It was a tumultuous night, the wind was blowing and the waves were leaping against the side of the boat. Suddenly, in the middle of the storm, Jesus appeared walking across the water toward their boat. When the disciples saw Him, they thought that He was a spirit and cried out in fear. But Jesus told them not to be afraid, that it was He who was coming toward them.

Peter was so thrilled that he cried out, "Lord, if it

be thou, bid me come unto thee on the water" (v. 28). The Bible tells us that Jesus simply said to him, "Come." And with that simple imperative as his command, Peter got out of the boat and walked on the water toward Jesus. This display of extraordinary faith on Peter's part was one of the disciple's most courageous acts. He was, in essence, saying, "Lord, if you can do it, then you can enable me to do it as well." With simple faith, he stepped out of the boat and walked on the water.

Peter had experienced many of the miracles of Jesus, but certainly none affected him more dramatically than this one. Peter was an impulsive and sanguine individual. He often spoke without thinking and was quick to act without considering the result. However, when his impetuousness was transformed into scriptural action, Peter was willing to take chances of faith that the other disciples were unwilling to take. There is no doubt in my mind that he was determined to follow Christ in every way possible. As a result, I think he learned a boldness and confidence that the other disciples often lacked.

CONFIDENCE IS BASED
UPON COMMITMENT

Determination is the result of commitment made by faith. Jesus spoke of that kind of commitment when He said, "If any man will come after me, let him deny himself, and take up his cross, and follow me" (Matthew 16:24). When we come to the point in our lives where we are willing to follow Jesus Christ with absolute abandon, we also will have come to the point where we do not care what anyone else other than Jesus Himself thinks about our commitment. We will no longer care what happens to our lives, except that they be lived in surrender to His will and purpose. We can overcome any obstacles, resolve any difficulties, and if necessary, move any mountains because we have made an absolute commitment of faith to Jesus Christ.

When Jesus spoke about "denying ourselves" and "taking up our cross," He knew well the level of commitment He was asking from those who would follow Him. He had been well acquainted with the cross, and what it meant, since childhood.

Josephus, the ancient historian, gives us the account of the Jewish wars that took place during the life of Jesus. He tells of one Roman garrison that was stationed in the little town called Sepphoris, which was located less than ten miles from Jesus' hometown. This garrison was placed in Sepphoris for the purpose of putting down a particular band of Jewish rebels in the region. The leader of these rebel soldiers was an outlaw by the name of Varus. This Varus was a skilled soldier, and in one mighty battle he led his small army to defeat the Romans and capture the fortress at Sepphoris.

When Rome heard of it, they sent a large military force to capture Varus and crush his guerilla band. Coming into Galilee with unparalleled strength, they overran the fortress at Sepphoris and captured Varus and two thousand of his soldiers.

Josephus goes on to tell us how the Romans, in order to make a lasting impression upon the Galileans, crucified the rebel soldiers. They took them one by one and put them upon crosses, not all together in one place, but scattered them in every direction throughout Galilee by the sides of the roads. As you walked the roads, you were never out of sight of a crucified rebel soldier, dying because he stood against the might of Rome. Furthermore, orders were given that they would not be cut down, but would have to rot upon their crosses!

Now think of the fact that Jesus saw this as a child. His disciples, and those whom He called to follow Him, doubtless remembered this as well. When Jesus said that if a person were going to follow Him, he was going to have to deny himself and take up his cross, both Jesus and those who heard Him understood the level of commitment of which He spoke.

Such commitment is greatly lacking in our world today. Yet, that kind of commitment, the willingness to bear one's cross if necessary, is the very key to finding personal confidence. When we are totally committed to a particular objective, we will always have the confidence to fulfill that commitment. Marriages which are successful survive because of commitment. Businesses which reach the pinnacle of success do so because of commitment. Without commitment, it is impossible to have the determination to make the sacrifices necessary to achieve our dreams.

How did Peter arrive at the kind of determination that led him to step out of the boat? He made that commitment because he had seen Jesus raise the dead, heal the sick, and transform the lives of sinners. He had seen Him calm the storms and defy nature itself. Therefore, Peter had absolute confidence in the supernatural, miracle-working power of the Lord Jesus.

Peter's commitment had already been settled in his own heart and mind. Once he heard Jesus' word of invitation, "Come," he responded immediately. How unlike many professing Christians today, who have heard the Word of God preached time and time again and are still reluctant to place their confidence in His miracle-working power to change their lives and see them through the seemingly insurmountable obstacles of life. When we really believe that the Bible means what it says, we will obey it every time. When we are convinced that God intends to stand by His promises, we will be able to trust those promises no matter what obstacles we face.

The greatest sin in the life of the average believer is one of omission, not commission. Most of us are careful about the sins we deliberately commit. Our biggest problem is neglecting the spiritual disciplines which are necessary to strengthen our daily lives. Failure to read the Word of God and to pray to the living God are just as serious as any deliberate acts committed against God. When we do not take time to spiritually refresh ourselves in the presence of the Lord, we will always lack spiritual confidence when we really need it.

There is something about faith which makes us move when God speaks. Whether He speaks to us through His Word or through a message at church or on a radio or television broadcast, we cannot help but respond to His powerful commands. The Spirit of God who dwells in us prompts us to respond in obedience to the Word of God. How long has it been since you have been moved at the request of God? How many times has God spoken to your heart about a particular matter and you failed to respond? Peter was so captivated by the power and person of Christ that he could not stay in the boat once Jesus bid him come to Him.

KEEP YOUR EYES ON JESUS

As long as Peter was captivated by Christ, he was able to walk on the water as if it were solid. His eyes were transfixed upon the Lord so that he never even noticed the storm raging about him. Peter did something for a few moments that no other human being had ever done before—he walked on the water and defied the laws of nature. But as soon as he took his eyes off the Lord and looked at the storm and the raging sea, he began to sink and nearly drowned.

New converts are the most excited people in the world. I love to be around young Christians. They add life, joy, and excitement to the fellowship of our church. While the spiritual elder statesmen who have known the Lord for a long time lend strength and stability to our congregation, the new converts add the balance of enthusiasm in their new-found walk with God. Many of them have been converted out of the most difficult and tragic situations a life could ever know. They are so grateful for the grace of God and the opportunity of forgiveness which they have found in Him, they are consumed with love for Jesus Christ. It shows on their faces and in their lives. They

eagerly get involved in almost every church activity—
Bible study, visitation, evangelism, and a host of other
things. To them, the Christian life is an adventure of
faith, and they are enjoying every moment of it. Like
Peter when he first stepped out of the boat, they have
their eyes fixed upon Christ so intently that the transformation that is taking place in their hearts is obvious
to everyone who knows them.

New converts are like little children, running up and
down the streets of the kingdom of God, enjoying
every new discovery that they make in the family of
God. I remember taking our children downtown,
along busy streets with traffic zooming past on every
side; they were fascinated by all the activity around
them. As they clung to my hand or to their mother's,
they had no fear because they were convinced that
they were safe with us. Our constant commitment to
Christ should result in the same kind of confidence—
one that enables us to walk through the storms of life
and know that we are safe with Him.

DON'T GIVE UP WHEN YOU FALL

While the account of Peter walking on the water is
one of the most amazing miracles in the Bible, verse 30
tells us that as soon as he took his eyes off the Lord and
focused on the tempest about him, he began to sink
and cried out for help. His fascination with faith suddenly became a fiasco. His venture onto the water revealed his vulnerability. Suddenly the miracle became
a mess!

While we may not literally walk on water, nevertheless, whenever we take a step of faith and trust God for the results and then begin to see those results, there will always be the temptation to refocus our attention on the negatives of life. Somewhere along the road of our spiritual journey we often begin to lose our initial fascination with the One who has transformed us, and we begin to spend more time looking at distractions than at our Savior. Once that happens, we are inevitably destined to collapse.

I cannot explain to you in technical or theological terms how this process develops. But in my own life and in my observation of others' lives, it inevitably happens whenever we spend more time on other things than we do on the things of God. Once that initial obsession to know Christ subsides, we begin to sink into the quagmire of self-interest and self-pity.

The prophet Isaiah reminds us that God keeps us in perfect peace when our minds are focused upon God. That is what the hymn writer Helen L. Lemmel meant when she wrote:

> *Turn your eyes upon Jesus,*
> *Look full in his wonderful face,*
> *And the things of earth will grow strangely dim,*
> *In the light of his glory and grace.* *

Peter's predicament began when he realized what he was doing. He had been walking on the water for

* "Turn Your Eyes Upon Jesus" by Helen H. Lemmel, copyright © 1922 by Singspiration Music/ASCAP. Renewed 1950. All rights reserved. Used by permission of the Benson Company, Inc., Nashville, TN.

several moments when he turned his focus from Jesus to the waves and storm, and immediately he began to sink. Once fear entered his heart, faith fled. It is the power of faith through a transformed mind that turns life's impossibilities into realities. The writer of the following poem points out the importance of right thinking:

> *If you think you are beaten, you are;*
> *If you think you dare not, you don't.*
> *If you want to win but don't think you can,*
> *It's almost a cinch you won't.*
>
> *If you think you'll lose, you're lost;*
> *For out in the world we find*
> *Success begins with a fellow's will:*
> *It's all in the state of mind.*
>
> *If you think you're outclassed, you are;*
> *You've got to think high to rise;*
> *You've got to be sure of yourself before*
> *You can ever win a prize.*
>
> *Life's battles don't always go*
> *To the stronger and faster man;*
> *But sooner or later the man who wins*
> *Is the man who thinks he can.*
>
> —*"Thinking," Walter D. Wintle*

Once a little town in the British Isles built a new jail which supposedly had an escape-proof cell. The great escape artist, Harry Houdini, was invited to come and see if he could escape from it.

The Great Houdini accepted the invitation. He had previously boasted that the jail had not been made that could hold him. On the appointed day, Houdini entered the cell and the jailer shut the door behind him. The great escape artist heard the noise of steel against steel as the jailer slipped the key into the lock. Once the jailer had gone, Houdini took out his tools and began to work on the cell door. An hour passed, then two. What had worked to open the locks on so many other doors didn't seem to be working on this one. Houdini couldn't understand; it had seemed so simple. Finally, after admitting defeat, Houdini leaned against the door in his fatigue—and the door opened! You see, the jailer had never locked it to begin with. The only place the door was locked was in the Great Houdini's mind!

Oh, that we might unlock our minds and allow God to do for us what He wants to do. It is only when we believe that God can and will work on our behalf that we will see Him transform the impossible into the possible. It is then that mountains move and people walk where they have never walked before. Set your mind right, and keep the Lord in sight.

GET UP AND TRY AGAIN

It would be unfair to Peter to end our observation of his story here. While it is true that he turned his eyes from the Lord and began to sink into the sea, it is also true that he cried out for help and was rescued. Like any desperate person, he cried, "Lord, save me." He had stepped out on faith and was so far from the boat that he was incapable of getting back to it by himself. In essence, he was saying, "Lord, if you don't save me, I won't make it." Just when it looked like he was about to go under, Christ moved in to meet his need.

Notice something that is often overlooked in this story. When Jesus reached out and took Peter by the hand, both of them walked on the water back to the boat! In reality, Peter walked on the water *twice* that day, once by himself and once hand-in-hand with his Lord. Peter not only got his eyes refocused on Christ, but he held on for all that he was worth.

Verse 32 tells us that as they stepped into the boat, the wind ceased and the storm ended. When we learn to walk with God by faith each step of the way, there will always come a time when the storms of life finally cease. The winds of trouble will not always blow against us. The raging torrents of life's great problems will not always overwhelm us. There will always come those moments of peace when we are back in the boat, safe and secure with the Lord who loves us.

The powerful lesson to be learned from this miracle of Peter walking on the water is the lasting confidence that God is with us both in the storms and in the calm. He is there when we are facing the difficulties of life, and He is also there when all is peaceful and serene. But whatever our situation, He will always be with us even unto the end of the journey. Peter got a dunking for his daring, but for a few moments he did something that none of the other disciples had ever done—he walked on the water. And before the day was over, he did it again; only this time he did it right. Though he still had many lessons of faith to learn, something had happened within Peter that he would never forget.

You, too, may be facing a serious decision which will take an incredible step of faith on your part. Put your confidence in God, focus your spiritual attention upon Him, and start walking with the confidence that He will be with you every step of the way!

4

THINGS UNLIMITED

■   ■   ■

*The Miracle of
Proper Perspective*

Mark 9:17–24

Mark 9:17-24

17   And one of the multitude answered and said, Master, I have brought unto thee my son, which hath a dumb spirit;

18   And wheresoever he taketh him, he teareth him; and he foameth, and gnasheth with his teeth, and pineth away: and I spake to thy disciples that they should cast him out; and they could not.

19   He answereth him, and saith, O faithless generation, how long shall I be with you? how long shall I suffer you? bring him unto me.

20   And they brought him unto him: and when he saw him, straightway the spirit tare him; and he fell on the ground, and wallowed foaming.

21   And he asked his father, How long is it ago since this came unto him? And he said, Of a child.

22   And ofttimes it hath cast him into the fire, and into the waters, to destroy him: but if thou canst do any thing, have compassion on us, and help us.

23   Jesus said unto him, If thou canst believe, all things are possible to him that believeth.

24   And straightway the father of the child cried out, and said with tears, Lord, I believe; help thou mine unbelief.

Jesus was a man of both compassion and power. He could love a sinner and banish a demon, all in the same breath. During his earthly ministry, He often did both, teaching His followers that much of the same power that He possessed could be theirs if they only had the proper perspective.

Mark 9:17–24 tells of a father with a son who was possessed by a devil. This devil often overtook the boy, throwing him to the ground. There the boy would wallow in the dirt and tear at his clothes. The father, of course, loved his son and was seeking someone to help him. Having heard of the disciples of Jesus and the miracles they had wrought, he sought them out. And although the disciples tried to cast out the devil and heal the boy, they could offer him no help. Finally, the man decided he would go to the very source of miracles, Jesus Himself.

"Jesus," he cried, "if thou canst do any thing, have compassion on us, and help us."

Jesus replied, "If thou canst believe, all things are possible to him that believeth!"

What a statement! Think for a moment about what Jesus was saying.

Jesus was telling this man that if he only truly believed, anything was possible. How wonderful to know that we serve an unlimited God, and yet, how often do we limit Him by our lack of faith? How often do we put limitations, not only on God, but on ourselves as His servants?

It is obvious we live in a pessimistic society. Ours is an "It can't be done" world. If you don't believe it, try going to work with a sparkling new idea; listen as those around you try to quench or squelch it. Even in many of our churches, in the very places God wants most to demonstrate His miracle power to the world, you will find little vision and excitement for what God can do.

I remember years ago when I was teaching my daughter Tonya the sixty-six books of the Bible. We were going through the Old Testament books, and as she got into the middle books, she said, "Isaiah . . . Jeremiah . . . Limitations . . ." "Whoa," I said, "back up and say that again." "All right, Daddy: Isaiah, Jeremiah, Limitations." I laughed and told her that the Bible book was not "Limitations" but "Lamentations." Later, I thought she might have had something there after all. I've seen many Christians who act as though they are living by the "book of Limitations" most of the time. But, there is no such book in the Word of God; God never wrote a book limiting Himself or His children. In fact, He wrote sixty-six books filled with un-limitations!

God has unlimited power to meet our needs. But we can limit that power with small-minded thinking. Only when we become willing to think and act in terms of those things which are unlimited will we be able to overcome the limitations that are being forced upon us daily.

DON'T LIMIT THE PEOPLE OF GOD

Jesus said, "All things are possible to him that believeth." Now, who did He say could do anything? Who did He say had all the possibilities? "Him that believeth." Who are the believers? The people of God. God doesn't say everything is possible to anybody; He says that all things are possible to those who believe. In Deuteronomy 7:6, God says this about His people: "For thou art a holy people unto the Lord thy God. The Lord thy God hath chosen thee to be a special people unto himself, above all the people that are on the face of the earth." God is talking about you, if you're a child of God. In Exodus 19:5, He says, "Therefore if you will obey my voice indeed, and keep my covenant, then ye shall be a peculiar treasure unto me, above all people, for all the earth is mine." In 1 John 3:1, the Bible says, "Behold, what manner of love the father hath bestowed upon us, that we should be called the Sons of God."

Look again at what He says we are: Sons of God, particular treasures, a special people. We have unlimited potential, but often we don't live like it. We live with the same pessimism, worry, frustrations, doubt, and struggles as those who don't know God. But God said we are special. He said we are His chosen people. Do you live like that? Do you live like you are a walking, talking, breathing child of God?

That doesn't mean that in and of ourselves we are better than anyone else; it simply means that we have been forgiven and given a position as God's children that we could never attain by ourselves. It doesn't mean we should go around with a "holier than thou" attitude, but that we should simply understand our position in Christ. There is nothing that degrades the kingdom of God more than people with a self-righteous attitude who condemn those who are outside the kingdom. That is called *pride*, and God says, "I hate it." He didn't just say that He didn't like it, but that He despised it.

There is a humorous story of a man who was so full of pride that his family got tired of living with him. He would get up every morning and look in the mirror and think about how good looking he was. When his wife could stand it no longer, she took the children and went to live with her mother. Eventually his pride got in the way of his work, and his boss fired him; even his dog ran away! Finally, he went to a psychologist and said, "Look, Doctor, I have a problem. People tell me I'm conceited; they say I have a terrible ego problem." The psychologist said, "Lie down on my couch and let's start from the very beginning." The man said, "All right. In the beginning, I created the heavens and the earth!"

Unfortunately, we have many people like that today. They almost think they are gods. It is true that we have become the sons of God; it is true we should realize who we are. But true Christianity will always be tempered by true humility. Were it not for the mercy and grace of Jesus Christ, we would be as lost as anyone could ever be. But because of our relationship with God, we are the children of God, and we have certain privileges Christ provides for us—we are a peculiar treasure and a special people. Therefore, we have unlimited potential because of what He has done for us.

Years ago while I was doing my undergraduate work in college, I attended a Head Start Program for children in downtown Atlanta. It was in a church with some wonderful black people. While there, I spent a lot of time observing one particular teacher. Every morning she would come in and say, "All right, children, say this: 'I am somebody.'" The little children would repeat, "I am somebody." "Say it again: 'I am somebody.'" She would continue this until every child firmly believed what they were saying.

This teacher was helping the children develop a proper self-concept. To understand that, indeed, they *were* somebody! I believe we can enter into the presence and the aura of God, not in pride or arrogance, but in simple humility and say, "Thank you, Lord, for through You we are somebody."

DON'T LIMIT THE PERSON OF GOD

There is a sense in which we limit God. We take the Creator God of the universe and try to conform Him to our small ideas of who He is. This not only limits our faith in God, it also keeps us from seeing Him as He *really* is. The Scriptures teach us that God will only react in response to faith. When we take the Creator God and reduce Him into a finite concept of what we think He is, we thwart His power in our behalf. God says, "All things are possible." Jesus said, "According to your faith, be it unto you." The degree to which we believe is the degree to which He will work in our lives.

How big is your God? The Bible gives witness of His

greatness in Psalm 19:1, "The heavens declare the glory of God, and the firmament showeth His handiwork." God has labored so that you and I could see how big He is. Consider the vastness of the heavens.

If you were to travel at the speed of light (which is 186,282 miles per second), in two seconds you would be past the moon. It would take you eight minutes to be past the sun. In four months, at 186,282 miles per second, you would leave our solar system. It would take you five years at that speed to reach the nearest star, Alpha-Centurion. If you wanted to exit from our galaxy (which is known as the Milky Way), it would take you one hundred thousand years. If you wanted to visit the next Galaxy, which is Great Nebuli, it would take you 1.5 million years. Yet you could travel at the speed of light for 4.5 billion years and never leave the universe.

Why did God build such a gigantic universe? He created it to declare His glory and to convince us of the magnitude of His power. Yet that same God who— holds this vast universe in the palm of His hand— knows us by name, feels each beat of our hearts, sees every tear that we shed, and hears our every prayer.

But so often we think God has to be harnessed and limited to our little concepts. We forget that Jesus said, "According to your faith . . . be it unto you." We look at the great men and women in the world today who seem to be able to move mountains by the power of their faith, and we wonder, "How do they do it?"

It's very simple. They serve a bigger God than we do! They don't place limitations on Him. Do you want to live a mountain-moving life? Do you want to face each day with confidence that victory is assured? Well then, remember that according to your faith be it unto you. It's conditional; we have to believe to such a degree that we stop limiting the person of God.

When I was a teenager, our local department store used to have a contest. If your name was drawn, you could either choose a small bicycle or you could reach into a jar filled with dollars and get as many as you could hold with your hand. Once my best friend won. I kept saying, "Ronnie, go for the dollars!" He said, "I want the bike." I said, "But look at your hands." He had big hands, with long fingers. "Go for the dollars!" Despite my pleas, he chose the little bike. I was amazed. He could have grabbed enough dollars to buy several bikes. Like many of us, he settled for less when he could have had more. God has all the riches of the universe for you, but it's only as big as the hand of faith that takes it.

DON'T LIMIT THE POWER OF GOD

Jesus promised, "All things are possible to him that believeth." If you believe and trust, you will not limit the power of God. The danger lies in underestimating the magnitude of the power of the God we have available to us. God has all power. Jesus Himself said, "All power is given unto me" (Matthew 28:18). We must not limit His power by our lack of faith.

One of the most exciting stories in God's Word is found in 2 Kings 6. It is the story of the prophet Elisha and his servant. Elisha had angered the King of Syria, who gathered his armies together and sent them to invade Israel. He sent them into Samaria to the town of Dothan to arrest the prophet. The troops marched out of Syria during the night and surrounded the little city of Dothan before sunrise. The Bible tells us that Elisha's servant got up early in the morning to do his chores. As he walked outside, he saw the mountains filled with soldiers and chariots, and his heart was suddenly stricken with fear.

Trembling in fear, the servant ran back into the house and told Elisha what he had seen. Elisha put on his garment, walked out, and looked about him. As he saw the troops surrounding the city, his heart leaped within him. Not because he saw them, but he saw something else! Turning to his servant standing beside him, he said "Don't be afraid! For our army is bigger than theirs!" (2 Kings 6:16, TLB). Elisha looked up to heaven and asked the Lord to open his servant's eyes that he might see. The Bible tells us the servant's eyes were opened, and, he saw the army of heaven with their horses and chariots of fire round about Elisha.

How often we limit the power of God with human eyesight that fails to see with the eyes of faith. We're not in this alone; we're surrounded by the armies of God. His power and resources are always available to us when we need them most.

DON'T LIMIT THE PURPOSE OF GOD

God has one great purpose for all people, and that is to lift them and bring them to Himself. The little boy we read about in Mark 9 is an example. He fell on the ground in front of Jesus and was wallowing, tearing at his clothes. Then as verse 27 tells us, "Jesus took him by the hand, and lifted him up; and he arose." The boy had been healed by the power of the Lord Jesus, in response to the faith of the boy's father. I can just imagine how faith must have become a great part of that family's home. The man and his son had come to Jesus pleading for help, but they had left with great faith in His miracle-working power. That is exactly what an encounter with God should always do for us. We should leave that encounter changed, different, and with a better understanding of our unlimited position in Him and His unlimited power to work in and through our lives.

Recently, one of our television viewers wrote me concerning this very thing. She evidently was a Christian, but was having a hard time with her own identity and her proper understanding of God. Perhaps you have experienced similar feelings.

Dear Dr. Lee:

I appreciate your recent message I heard over our local television station dealing with the bigness of God. I'm a young mother of two small children who is going through a terrible divorce. My husband left me for another woman about three months ago and my heart feels like it's about to break apart. I have always pictured myself as a decent-looking person and have always tried to keep myself pretty nice for my husband. I guess that didn't work, though. I guess he saw something in his new girlfriend that I just didn't have. Maybe I just didn't have what it took to begin with.

Pastor, what can I do? I want to believe God is big enough to help me and get my kids and me through this problem, I really do, but I really wonder if anyone is that great—even God. Please help me to understand about God. I've just got to have somebody's help.

Sincerely,

Debbie

As I read Debbie's letter, I understood perfectly. At one time or another, we have all found ourselves in some dark valley of despair and have wondered in our hearts if God was really big enough to rescue us. Not that we were doubting Him, nor insulting His greatness; it was just that, at that moment, our problems seemed so big that they overshadowed our faith and distorted our vision of the eternal God.

But what are we to do? When our perspectives are too small, how can we enlarge them? This illustration may provide an answer.

Recently I was driving across the Nevada desert. There was little to be seen except for the tumbleweed and sand. Suddenly, what looked to be a small hill appeared on the horizon in front of me. I thought, "Well, since I've been driving so long, when I reach that little hill, I'll climb it just for the exercise." On and on I drove, trying to reach that distant hill. After an hour, I finally reached it, except that what I had been seeing was not a hill after all—it was a mountain!

What had caused me to think that this mountain was so small? Nothing more than an error in perspective caused by the distance I was from it. The reason God is small to many people is that they are not near to Him. The nearer we get, the greater we find Him to be.

Never limit the people of God, the person of God, the power and purpose of God in and for your life. When we do, we simply destroy His ability to do that which He has promised. Remember the words of Jesus, "If thou canst believe, all things are possible to him that believeth" (Mark 9:23).

5

FAITH FOR
THE DAY OF
DESPERATION

■　■　■

The Miracle of Faith

Mark 5:22–23, 35–42

22   And, behold, there cometh one of the rulers of the synagogue, Jairus by name; and when he saw him, he fell at his feet,

23   And besought him greatly, saying, My little daughter lieth at the point of death: I pray thee, come and lay thy hands on her, that she may be healed; and she shall live.

. . . .

35   While he yet spake, there came from the ruler of the synagogue's house certain which said, Thy daughter is dead; why troublest thou the Master any further?

36   As soon as Jesus heard the word that was spoken, he saith unto the ruler of the synagogue, Be not afraid, only believe.

37   And he suffered no man to follow him, save Peter, and James, and John the brother of James.

38   And he cometh to the house of the ruler of the synagogue, and seeth the tumult, and them that wept and wailed greatly.

39   And when he was come in, he saith unto them, Why make ye this ado, and weep? the damsel is not dead, but sleepeth.

40   And they laughed him to scorn. But when he had put them all out, he taketh the father and the mother of the damsel, and them that were with him, and entereth in where the damsel was lying.

41   And he took the damsel by the hand, and said unto her, Talitha cumi; which is, being interpreted, Damsel, (I say unto thee,) arise.

42   And straightway the damsel arose, and walked; for she was of the age of twelve years. And they were astonished with a great astonishment.

I was walking down the aisle one Sunday night on my way to the pulpit when suddenly someone grabbed my arm. As I turned, I found myself looking into the anguished face of a middle-aged man.

"Pastor, I'm desperate!" he pleaded, "I need to see you as soon as possible."

As we talked in my office that night after the evening service, Tom explained that his wife, Jan, was leaving him after nearly twenty years of marriage.

"I just don't understand it," Tom said, hanging his head and weeping bitterly. "I have tried everything I know to do to get her to stay, and I just don't know where else to turn."

"I'm sure there are many problems in your marriage which need to be resolved," I responded. "But I am also sure that if there was ever a time that you needed a miracle of faith, it is certainly now!"

All of us have times in our lives when we become desperate, when we come to the realization that things are out of our control. Perhaps it's when death threatens to take a loved one from us, or our spouse leaves, or we lose a job, or our health fails. At such times, we are pushed to the point where we can no longer control our own destiny. We are used to feeling that we can make our own decisions and decide our own fate. But when the bottom falls out of our lives, that terrible feeling of helplessness gets our complete attention.

61

No matter how long you have known the Lord or how far you have walked in your spiritual pilgrimage, when crisis comes, desperation often sets in. When a husband runs off with another woman and leaves his wife to raise their children by herself, she will always face desperation. She must then make difficult and sometimes desperate choices regarding the support, education, and even the very future of her children.

Desperation is often only a telephone call or visit to the doctor away. Suddenly, the normal pattern of life is torn apart, and we who were so confident that everything was fine find ourselves facing desperate alternatives. In such cases, even the best of people will begin to panic.

Mark 5 tells the story of a desperate man whose name was Jairus. He was a man of education, of fame and fortune, and a ruler in the synagogue. But despite his material possessions and social position, something happened in his life over which he had no control: his daughter became sick "unto death." In desperation, Jairus decided to go to Jesus and ask for His help. The Bible tells us that he came to Christ and fell at His feet and begged Him to come and lay hands on his daughter that she might live.

Jairus was a man whose well-ordered lifestyle had suddenly been thrown into chaos. He was a man of distinction who had become a man of dilemma. In that state of despair, he reached out to Jesus with the kind of faith which God rewarded.

THE CALL FOR HELP

The first step in expressing desperate faith is to call for help. Such faith must be openly and clearly expressed; it cannot be kept to yourself. We do not know whether Jairus was a secret believer in Christ prior to this event or one who may have openly professed faith in Him. If he were like most of the Jewish leaders of that day, however, it is unlikely that he had made any kind of public profession of faith. Chances are it was only when he was faced with a desperate choice that Jairus publicly declared his faith in Christ alone to meet his need. He did not write his request on a piece of paper and slip it into Jesus' hand, nor did he send someone else to deliver the request for him. Rather, he openly and publicly verbalized his desperate faith when he told Jesus that if He would lay His hands upon his daughter, he knew that she would be healed. Jairus stated his faith so that all the world could hear, and we are still hearing him nearly two thousand years later.

Desperate faith is bold and direct. When we get into a situation where we must have God's help, we suddenly learn how to put our faith into action. This was exactly the case with Jairus, who threw himself at the Savior's feet and called out for help.

We must learn to approach Christ in the same manner in which this ruler of the Jews came to Him. It is not enough to know who Jesus is, or what He potentially can do for us. We must understand that Christ alone can meet our needs, and then we must come to Him openly, in complete and total faith, expressing that faith and acknowledging those needs.

On a recent trip to Africa, I spent a day with King Goodwill, the King of the Zulu nation. I had never before met a king face to face. The palace where I was received was fascinating; skins of lions and tigers filled each room, as well as trophies from the king's many hunts. After formal greeting, we were ushered into a formal meeting room where the king was seated upon his throne and I was seated in a chair at his side. As various servants arrived, they would kneel at the threshold of the entrance and wait for him to bid them to enter the room. When they did, they would come across the room on their knees, with their heads bowed. After receiving their orders, they would back out of the room on their knees as well.

I had never seen anything quite like it. I could not imagine that an earthly king received such obedient servitude in this day and age. When I asked the king why the servants approached him on their knees, he said, "Sir, in our land no one stands in the presence of the king." As I sat there considering how much ceremony was being paid to an earthly king, I began to realize how much more respect should be given to Jesus Christ, who is King of Kings and Lord of Lords. It is no wonder that when He appeared in Scripture, people fell down at His feet as though they were dead. Even Isaiah, the greatest of the prophets, cried out, "Woe is me!" as he knelt before the Lord (Isaiah 6:5).

We live in a world that is too busy to take time to acknowledge the person and authority of Jesus Christ. We have time for everything else and everyone else except Him. But the Bible reminds us that there will come a time when every knee shall bow and every tongue confess that He is Lord (Philippians 2:10–11).

Desperate faith which cries out to God for help is faith which recognizes that He alone can help us. He alone is King of all, and all power is in His hands. It is that expression of confidence which turns our attention toward the One who alone can meet our needs.

OVERCOMING DOUBTS

Whenever we cry out to God in desperate faith, there will always be the need for that faith to overcome the obstacles of doubt. We are told that after Jairus made his request to Jesus, others came from the synagogue to announce that his daughter was already dead. No sooner had the ruler expressed his plea, when word reached him of his daughter's seemingly hopeless condition. But Jairus remained steadfast in his confidence that, even in the face of death, Christ could miraculously intervene on his daughter's behalf.

Perhaps you have had a time in your life when you trusted God for something, and you were so excited that you were bursting with joy, yet someone tried to cast a doubt on your newfound faith and confidence. It seems that the greater our faith, the greater the chances are that doubters will try to diminish it. Often those who discourage us the most are not our enemies, but our friends. It may be that the people who love us the most encourage us the least. At the very time we need a greater faith in Christ, they are the very ones who may discourage our faith by pointing out the obstacles in our path.

Sometimes even other believers try to discourage our faith because they are afraid that it is too radical and will get us into trouble. Perhaps it is because they do not understand the great power of faith itself. In our human rationale, we tend to want to believe that God has left us to our own devices and that He will not move on our behalf. The tragedy is that when we get ourselves into such a condition, God *won't* move on our behalf.

When Moses sent out the twelve spies of Israel into the land of Canaan, they all agreed that the land "flowed with milk and honey." They all recognized that what God has promised in regard to the goodness of the land was true. However, ten of the twelve brought a negative report, and announced that the people were so great and powerful that the Israelites were "like grasshoppers in their sight." Only Joshua and Caleb brought a positive report and had faith to believe that God could enable them to conquer this land.

It is unlikely that Moses deliberately chose the most pessimistic people that he could find for this task. No doubt, he chose what he thought to be the twelve best men that he had. These were men in whom he had confidence and whose word he wanted to believe. But when they came back announcing that the task was impossible and doubting the promises of God, Moses was left with the terrible consequences of their negative attitude.

Whenever you find yourself in a desperate situation which calls for desperate faith, do not be surprised if there are those who doubt that such faith will do you any good. There are always doubters in every circumstance of life. The real miracle of faith occurs when we allow our faith to overcome our doubts. Our greatest spiritual victories will often come at the very point of our deepest discouragement. If anyone ever had a reason to give up, it was certainly Jairus. However, he had such confidence in Jesus that his faith remained fixed on Him, in spite of the circumstances. Jairus overcame the threat of doubt and so can you. Whenever you are facing life's most desperate moments, remember to keep your confidence focused on Christ alone.

ENCOURAGING OTHERS

When Jesus heard the report of the girl's death and saw the look of concern on Jairus' face, He said, "Be not afraid. Only believe" (v. 36). By commanding his belief, Jesus drew Jairus' attention to the most important principle in life, the potential of the miracle of faith.

Christ announced that the girl was not dead, but merely sleeping (which was a typical Jewish euphemism for death). What the Lord meant by this was that, though she really was dead, He intended to raise her back to life. The text goes on to tell us that the bystanders laughed Him to scorn and insisted that the girl really was dead. This underscores the greatness of the miracle which was about to occur: no one who doubted the reality of her death could doubt the reality of the miracle of faith which occurred when He raised her back to life. Jesus immediately went to Jairus' home and dispersed the mourners and doubters and dealt with the girl Himself!

Whenever we face the difficult struggles of life, and there are those who would cause us to doubt and despair, we must turn our attention to Christ alone and let all others be dispersed. Our Lord literally threw them out of the house, and we must often do the same. If God is saying anything to us today from this passage, it is, "Don't let the doubters discourage you!"

Whenever we face difficult decisions in life, God's grace is always available to help us overcome our doubts. He is there to encourage us. He wants us to use our response to Him in faith to encourage others to do the same, just as Jairus' initial faith may have inspired many people to come to faith in Christ. Because Jairus was willing to believe, God was able to display His great power and point others to the miraculous nature of His Son.

One of the things that has always struck my attention in this passage is the great compassion of Jesus. Our

Lord could have legitimately responded in any one of a number of ways to this request. But whenever He was touched by the sincere faith and desperate pleas of individuals seeking His help, Christ always moved with compassion to help them. While He was on this earth, our Lord could not turn a deaf ear or a blind eye to the sufferings and tragedies of others. Time after time, He reached out to meet the needs of those who did not even deserve His help. Such is the picture of His great grace which continues to reach out to us today. While we may be removed some twenty centuries from this scene, we are reminded that it is the same quality of faith which moves God on our behalf today.

I once sat with a young couple in my office one Sunday afternoon, encouraging them to submit their lives to Christ in an act of faith and commitment. As we talked together, the husband looked at me and asked, "What will my friends think if I do this?"

My response was, "They may very well come to faith in Christ themselves!"

Three weeks later they brought another couple to me and explained that they, too, wanted to come to Christ. Whenever we respond by faith to God's dealings in our hearts, He will not only encourage us personally, but He will also use our responsive faith to encourage others to trust Him as well.

GETTING RESULTS

When Jesus arrived at Jairus' house, He entered the little girl's room, took her by the hand, and said, "Little girl, I say to you, arise. And immediately the girl arose and walked" (v. 41, NKJV). Jesus acted in the power of His authority when He said, "I say to you. . . ." He alone has the supreme authority over our lives and over all of life's situations.

We cannot imagine the joy that her father experienced when the little girl arose from her death bed and walked away! One act of desperate faith which Christ honored resulted in unparalleled joy on two levels: the miracle of resurrection when a young girl was brought back to life and the even greater miracle of faith wrought in the heart of a father who learned that he could trust the Savior even in life's most desperate moment.

There is no difficulty which is beyond the limits of God's power and grace! Whatever problems we may be facing right now, whatever tough times we may be going through, Christ has all the love and power that we need to face them. There is no better time than the present to put our faith and trust in Him who alone can meet our needs.

There is a verse in 2 Chronicles that has always been very special to me in my moments of desperation: "For the eyes of the Lord run to and fro throughout the whole earth, to show himself strong in the behalf of them whose heart is perfect toward him" (2 Chronicles 16:9). When I read that, and with a pure heart come into His presence claiming that promise, He has always, always shown Himself strong in my behalf. Just as Jesus responded to the miracle of faith within the heart of Jairus, likewise He will do the same if He finds faith in our hearts toward Him.

6

HOW TO HANDLE YOUR MOMENT OF CRISIS

■ ■ ■

The Miracle of Hope

Daniel 6:18–23

Daniel 6:18-23

18   Then the king went to his palace, and passed the night fasting: neither were instruments of music brought before him: and his sleep went from him.

19   Then the king arose very early in the morning, and went in haste unto the den of lions.

20   And when he came to the den, he cried with a lamentable voice unto Daniel: and the king spake and said to Daniel, O Daniel, servant of the living God, is thy God, whom thou servest continually, able to deliver thee from the lions?

21   Then said Daniel unto the king, O king, live for ever.

22   My God hath sent his angel, and hath shut the lions' mouths, that they have not hurt me: forasmuch as before him innocency was found in me; and also before thee, O king, have I done no hurt.

23   Then was the king exceeding glad for him, and commanded that they should take Daniel up out of the den. So Daniel was taken up out of the den, and no manner of hurt was found upon him, because he believed in his God.

Recently I returned to the Atlanta airport after a heavy speaking schedule in another city. Tired and anxious to get home to my family, I hurriedly made my way through the crowds to the baggage claim and then across the parking deck to my car. It seemed as though I couldn't walk fast enough. Suddenly, however, out of the corner of my eye, I caught something that made me pause and forget myself. There, upon the wall of the parking deck, someone had taken time to scribble the words: I JUST CAN'T TAKE IT ANYMORE.

As I walked away, I wondered who had taken time in this busy airport to write their heart upon a wall. Perhaps it was some businessman who had had enough of the pressures at work. Perhaps it was a battered and abused wife. Or maybe it was a teenager whose parents never took time to understand his problems and who, in one final, futile cry for help, wrote upon the wall of a parking deck: I JUST CAN'T TAKE IT ANYMORE. As I walked away, I realized that more than likely I would never know who wrote those words, but one thing was certain: Whoever wrote those words was facing a moment of crisis.

Each of us has a different perspective on how we define a crisis in our lives. For some, it is nothing more than breaking a fingernail or finding that our brand new car will not start in the morning. All of us face these little aggravating crises which generally do not amount to much. However, if we allow the little things to get us down, we will never be able to deal with the real major crises of life which are bound to come our way.

A real crisis is one of great proportion—the kind which is totally unexpected and takes us by the heels, turns us upside down, and shakes us so hard that it leaves us clinging to life itself. It is during those kinds of crises that God works most powerfully in our lives.

EVERY CRISIS IS AN OPPORTUNITY

Every time we face a crisis, we are also facing an opportunity to grow in our relationship with God and providing Him with the opportunity to bring us through one of life's difficult moments. A crisis can also push us to the brink of spiritual collapse. In each moment of crisis, there is both the opportunity for growth and the potential for failure; either is possible. Our response determines whether or not it becomes a building block or a stumbling stone in our lives.

Whenever I think of someone in a moment of crisis, I am always reminded of Daniel in the lion's den in Babylon. The story recorded in Daniel 6 tells us that the Persians had recently conquered Babylon, and a new Persian king, Darius the Mede, had been installed to rule over the city on behalf of the Emperor of Persia. Daniel was a Jew, living in exile during the Babylonian captivity. He had served faithfully under the Babylonian administration and was now confronted with the issue of service under the new Persian administration. Originally taken captive many years earlier as a teenager, Daniel had risen to power and influence under the Babylonian Nebuchadnezzar. However, by the time he was thrown into the lion's den, Daniel was in his eighties.

The Bible tells us that many of the other exiles and servants of the Persian government hated Daniel because of his faithful commitment to the Lord. These rivals eventually persuaded King Darius to pass a decree that no one be allowed to pray to any deity or king other than himself for thirty days. By playing upon the king's pride and arrogance, they were able to persuade him to threaten anyone who would not comply with this law with the penalty of certain death. Darius signed the law into effect without realizing its implications for his trusted servant, Daniel. When Daniel heard the decree of the law read, he determined in his heart to continue to pray unto the Lord his God. In fact, Daniel threw open the windows of his room and openly prayed unto the Lord. He was eventually arrested and charged before the king with violating this law. Though Darius was saddened, he nevertheless ordered Daniel to be thrown into the den of lions.

Here was a man who was facing the biggest crisis of his life. He had not only lost his job, been rejected by his friends, and accused by his enemies, but he was now facing certain death. In those times, the lions kept for such purposes were often starved and tormented so they would immediately devour whoever or whatever was placed in their den.

Compared to Daniel's situation, most of us really don't have many crisis moments at all. But for those that we do have, we, too, can have hope that God will lead us through. The God who rescued Daniel from the den of lions is the same God who cares for His children today.

TROUBLE IN THE MAKING

Everyone faces trouble sooner or later. Being a Christian does not automatically make us immune to crises. While our relationship with Christ certainly ought to help us face our problems more effectively, it does not guarantee a crisis-free life. In fact, the Bible virtually promises us that we are going to have troubles. Jesus Himself said, "In the world ye shall have tribulation" (John 16:33). The word *tribulation* (Greek, *thlipsis*) means "affliction, persecution, or trouble." The original Greek word is derived from the root word for "narrow," which implies the kind of trouble that is such that one narrowly escapes its consequences. This in turn implies the idea of a crisis which could bring us to the very brink of disaster.

While the Bible clearly teaches that we will often face trouble in our lives, it is also clear that we do not have to go out of our way to look for it. Nobody enjoys trouble; most of us will go out of our way to avoid it. However, there are always a few people who seem to enjoy having trouble and talking about their troubles.

Little children enjoy showing off the Band-Aids that their mothers put over their cuts and scrapes as a way of drawing attention from their peers and words of affection from adults. They do it because it makes them noticed when otherwise they might not be.

Some people are like that. They seem to enjoy being afflicted because it gives them something to talk about. However, most of us want to avoid trouble, not court it.

For most of us, a crisis generally comes unexpectedly; it is not something for which we can plan or prepare. In fact, the greatest crises of life tend to come at the most inopportune times. The telephone rings in the middle of the night, and you are told the awful news of some tragedy. Or your doctor explains that you have a serious illness. While we have no guarantee for tomorrow, the great promise of Scripture is that we can have *hope* for today.

As a pastor, I have seen lives that were permanently changed in one day as the result of some personal tragedy. At these times, we are left almost speechless. I often think of Job's three friends who came to comfort him in his moment of agony and could only sit there in abject silence. It is not easy to be a pastor at such times. I naturally want to say something of comfort and encouragement, but I am also concerned that I not say something trite or inappropriate. Grief is such that it needs to be properly expressed and understood as a normal response to such crises.

There are basically two types of crises with which most of us must deal. The first is the kind which has permanent consequences, like the death of a loved one. The other is the kind that has ongoing effects, such as a serious accident or illness. In either case, the Bible gives us words of wisdom and raises a banner of hope for the future.

One of the most basic promises in Scripture is found in Romans 8:28: "And we know that all things work together for good to them that love God, to them who are the called according to his purpose." This is a reminder that no matter what trouble comes our way or how severe it may be, God can still turn it around for His glory and honor.

The Christian life is one of facing problems, not running from them. In our greatest moments of trouble, we need not fear nor panic because the power of God's Spirit in us will enable us to meet any crisis.

There are four specific steps which are essential in dealing with life's crises.

1. Let your crisis help you discover who you really are.

Whenever we are shaken by life's situations, whatever falls out is what we really are. By that I mean that when we are squeezed by the pressures of life, whatever comes out of us at that moment is indicative of what is really inside us in the first place. Someone once asked me, "What comes out of an orange when you squeeze it?" My natural response was to say, "Orange juice." To which he responded, "No, whatever is in the orange will come out . . . seeds and all!"

Whenever we are squeezed by life's pressures, whatever comes out of our lives is an evidence of what is within us. Sometimes predictable responses come out; at other times, the most unexpected reactions occur. In a moment of crisis, some people seem able to rise to the occasion and meet it with greater confidence and assurance than even they thought possible. Others seem to collapse under the pressure. A person can appear to have everything in life under control until trouble comes. Then everything falls apart!

When our Lord announced that the disciples would forsake Him and flee, Peter insisted that he would never forsake Him. When Jesus warned him that he would not only forsake Him, but also deny Him, Peter insisted that would never happen. But later that night when Jesus was arrested and taken to stand trial before the Sanhedrin, Peter violently denied that he ever knew Him. In the moment of crisis, when accusing fingers were being pointed at him, Peter panicked and denied the very Lord whom he claimed to serve. Only in that moment of failure did he realize his own personal weakness. Unfortunately, some of us never fully understand who we are until the time of testing comes.

Certainly Peter was under tremendous pressure to compromise his beliefs. Undoubtedly, circumstances were against him at that moment. But the Scripture reminds us that circumstances do not *make us* what we are, they merely *reveal* what we are. Peter failed because of a personal weakness in his own character. In every crisis I believe there is a peak, a moment of decision, that reveals to us our inward self.

In contrast to Peter, Daniel, who was also under tremendous pressure to compromise his belief, stood firm in his commitment to God. He had already faced some serious threats in his lifetime, but he had never before been threatened with being thrown to the lions. Yet, fully understanding the fate that awaited him, Daniel abandoned himself to God. He opened his windows, knelt down, and prayed out loud so that all could hear him. In so doing, he was making public his profession of faith in God alone. Crisis or no crisis, Daniel stood his ground. As he did, it became clear, not only to him, but to everyone else, what a man of conviction Daniel really was. I've heard it said:

> *Dare to be a Daniel,*
> *Dare to stand alone.*
> *Dare to have a purpose firm,*
> *Dare to make it known.*

It is in life's trying moments that we gain a greater insight as to our own strengths and weaknesses, and we must be willing to learn the lesson of personal assessment. If a crisis reveals an area of need in your life, don't run away from it. Face it, and determine to profit from your mistake. If the crisis reveals a strength and determination greater than you may have realized, thank God for it, but take no credit for it. Ultimately our spiritual strength comes from God Himself, not from within ourselves.

2. Let your crisis force you to God.

In every time of trouble, there is one particular point of decision that seems to determine our destiny for the future. It is at that point our faith is tested the most. We can either allow our problems to make us bitter or better—the choice is up to us!

There is a precarious balance of truth here. On one hand, God is sovereignly in control of the events and circumstances of our lives; nothing happens to us apart from His will and purpose for us. But on the other hand, we still have a personal responsibility and accountability to obey the directions of His will as revealed in His Word.

I have never been able to fully understand why people turn their backs on God at the very moment they need Him the most. It is in our hour of trouble that we need to call upon the Lord because that is especially when He has promised to be there to meet our needs.

It is unlikely that Daniel was experienced in dealing with lions. The Bible says that Daniel survived the lions'-den ordeal because "he believed in his God" (v. 23). Based on the concepts we have already seen taught in Scripture, it is fair to assume that Daniel literally trusted himself to the sovereignty of God. He allowed himself no other choice but to throw himself on the mercy and grace of God. In his moment of crisis, Daniel turned to God for help.

Again, I can't help but think of Job who never once turned away from God though he was bombarded with one crisis after another. Who among us has ever had the kind of problems he had? He lost all of his children and all his possessions in one day. If that were not enough, he lost his health the next day. As the book of Job opens, we find him sitting in a pile of ashes, scrapping his boils and blisters with broken pieces of pottery. Even his wife and friends turned against him. His wife suggested that he may as well curse God and die! His friends accused him of harboring some secret sin in his life which had incurred the wrath of God. But Job's faith remained steadfast in the Lord. "Though he slay me, still will I trust him!" he proclaimed.

As it was with Daniel, likewise the crisis in Job's life revealed the depth of his character and drove him closer to God. Through a lengthy process of self-evaluation and spiritual assessment, Job realized that he had no human wisdom or resources to solve his own problems. In total faith and confidence he cast himself upon the grace of God. This may seem to be an act of utter desperation, but in reality, it was an act of total faith and confidence.

Troubles may come into our lives, but desperation need not overtake us. For when the greatest difficulties of life confront us, they will always remind us that there is a source of strength beyond ourselves which is far greater than we could ever have imagined. When the crises of life turn our attention heavenward, those troubles will actually become part of the process of our spiritual growth.

3. Let your crisis become a testimony of God's grace.

Whenever we face the difficulties of life, we need to remember that others are watching us. Husband, wife, child, friend, or relative—someone is watching your life right now! It's not so much your reaction when things are going smoothly that they will notice, but whether or not you remain faithful to Christ when all else has apparently gone wrong. While we do not try to bring such difficulties upon ourselves, and don't even anxiously anticipate their coming into our lives, we must recognize that when they do come, God can use them as a testimony to speak to others. Our faith says to them, "God brought me through my difficulties, and He can do the same for you."

In Daniel's moment of crisis, he displayed not only his confidence in God, but he displayed his God to the world as well. When Daniel was miraculously spared from the den of lions and released the following morning, King Darius announced, that men should "tremble and fear before the God of Daniel: for his is the living God" (v. 26). Darius himself may or may not have come to personal faith in the living God, but from that point on he certainly knew who God was! Daniel's faith was a testimony of God's grace and power. It impressed the king and stunned a nation. Whenever we read such accounts in Scripture, we need to remember that our testimonies are not lived in isolation. Our lives are always lived in the crucible of human relationships. In our moments of crisis, God is speaking through our very responses of faith to the hearts and lives of those who know us best.

4. Blessings always follow crises.

After Daniel's miraculous deliverance from the den of lions, he was promoted by Darius and prospered throughout his reign. The Babylonians believed in a concept of trial by ordeal in which a person was placed into a difficult situation from which he could not humanly escape. If, however, he survived the ordeal, the Babylonians assumed that he was innocent and that the gods had spared him. Based upon this belief, Darius had to have been impressed that Daniel's innocence had been vindicated, and he elevated him to a position of even greater leadership.

Likewise, after all of Job's sufferings, the Bible tells us that God doubled the blessing on his life. While we are going through a crisis, it is often difficult to see the good that will result from it. When it has passed, and it will, the blessings of God will be abundant upon our behalf.

There was once a young man by the name of Joseph Scriven who had fallen deeply in love with a beautiful girl. He was so infatuated with her love and taken with her beauty that all he could think of was her. They fell in love, and planned to marry. However, the day before their wedding, the girl drowned in a boating accident. Young Joseph Scriven was distraught with bitterness and despair. For months he questioned the wisdom and purpose of God. Then, after many days of agony, he realized that he had no one to turn to but God Himself to regain the peace of mind that he so desperately sought. So his heart finally returned to fellowship and trust in God. Later, Joseph Scriven sat down and wrote the words of this familiar hymn of hope:

> *What a friend we have in Jesus,*
> *All our sins and griefs to bear,*
> *What a privilege to carry,*
> *Everything to God in prayer.*
> *Oh, what peace we often forfeit,*
> *Oh, what needless pain we bear,*
> *All because we do not carry,*
> *Everything to God in prayer.*

7

LET LOVE CHANGE
YOUR LIFE

■　　■　　■

The Miracle of Love

Acts 9:1–6

Acts 9:1–6

1 And Saul, yet breathing out threatenings and slaughter against the disciples of the Lord, went unto the high priest,

2 And desired of him letters to Damascus to the synagogues, that if he found any of this way, whether they were men or women, he might bring them bound unto Jerusalem.

3 And as he journeyed, he came near Damascus: and suddenly there shined round about him a light from heaven:

4 And he fell to the earth, and heard a voice saying unto him, Saul, Saul, why persecutest thou me?

5 And he said, Who art thou, Lord? And the Lord said, I am Jesus whom thou persecutest: it is hard for thee to kick against the pricks.

6 And he trembling and astonished said, Lord, what wilt thou have me to do? And the Lord said unto him, Arise, and go into the city, and it shall be told thee what thou must do.

One of the top songs on the pop charts of the 1980s—"What's Love Got to Do with It?"— poses the question "What's love but a secondhand emotion?" Shortly after its release, that song became the number one song in the country.

When I first heard it, I couldn't help but wonder if that is our nation's view of love. Do we really think that love is no more than a secondhand emotion? If so, we have some real educating to do concerning the truth about real love.

The apostle Paul learned his lesson about love. In his encounter with Christ on the road to Damascus, love changed his life forever. In Acts 9 we find the story of the man Scripture introduces by saying, "He went about breathing out threatenings and slaughter against the disciples of the Lord."

Paul, in his persecution of the Christians, was a cold, hardhearted, merciless man. He was also recorded as being at the stoning of Stephen, and some attribute him as being the leader of the mob. But later in the New Testament, it is evident something had happened in his life. Here he is seen as a man who had a heart of deep compassion. Perhaps of all those in the New Testament, besides the Lord Jesus, Paul demonstrated more love than anyone else. How could such a change have taken place?

Acts 9:1–6 gives us the answer: how Paul, on his way to persecute believers, was struck to the ground by a light from heaven and had a miraculous encounter with Christ. At that moment, Paul became a man of love. It's hard to conceive that one so full of hatred could be changed into one so full of love in a moment's time, but nevertheless it's true.

Perhaps you can identify with that. You may be bitter because someone has hurt you. Or, you may feel it has been so long since you have loved anyone that you may have forgotten how to love. Well, there is good news for you. The same power that changed Paul's life is still available today. Give God a chance, and see what He will do by the power of His love in your heart.

LOVE WILL CHANGE YOU OUTWARDLY

Paul was a prime example of the way love will change how you respond outwardly. Throughout his life, prior to his decision for Jesus, Paul was centered on himself. He went to study that he might become part of the Sanhedrin. He gloried in his knowledge. And he sought to elevate himself through his adherence to the Jewish law. His entire life was centered on self.

Paul went about persecuting Christians, slaying them and dragging them off to jail. Why? That he might work his way up in the political structure of the Jews. All of that was for self. But once he met Jesus, his eyes went from self to the Cross, then to others.

Jesus changes one's focus. When a person really has an encounter with Christ, his focus is changed from one who elevates himself to one who cares about others. He changes from a person who says, "What can it do for me?" to a person who says, "What can I do for you?"

In Romans 9:3, Paul said that he would even be willing to be estranged from Jesus for the cause of the Jews. A man who heretofore had only considered himself now says he would give up his relationship with Jesus, though it would cost him eternity, if the Jews would just accept Jesus as Savior.

Jesus described this kind of love in John 3:16, "For God so loved the world, that He gave his only begotten Son, that whosoever believeth in him should not perish, but have everlasting life." That word *whosoever* is undeniably linked to the very heart of Scripture. It is dear to the heart of God Himself. Not that God would profit—but "whosoever." Paul had been transformed from looking out for himself to looking out for others. That kind of transformation can only be brought about by God.

A survey done by national advertisers revealed that the most important question on the minds of the American public is, "What's in it for me?"

Many of us, I'm afraid, are like the boy who went down to the movie theater to get a job. The manager took him into the dark theater and said, "Now, son, all of these people in here will be your responsibility. Let me give you a little test before I hire you. If a fire broke out in this theater, and you were in charge of all these people what would you do?" The boy replied, "Mister, you don't have to worry about me. I can take care of myself!"

Selfish thinking has become the basic attitude of most Americans. It is the cause of personal conflicts, material pursuits, and marital breakup. Have you ever heard someone say, "I believe I'll divorce this person because I think it's for their own good?" Instead you hear, "We can't live together because we're incompatible." Or, another classic reply is "I need this divorce. It's really the best thing for me."

Why do women abort tiny little babies when there are millions of couples who can't have children, whose hearts are aching for a child they can love? Because they say, "I don't want to be bothered. I don't want to go through it. What's in it for me?"

What is the basic attitude of the pornographer or the person who is obsessed by pornography? "What's in it for me? I want to feed my lust."

Why do terrorists blow airplanes out of the sky with innocent people on board? Why would they risk their lives to destroy the lives of others? Because they say, "We want to propagate our theology, our philosophy. It's going to be our way—or nobody's way! Let the world die. We only want what we want for ourselves."

Although this may be the typical American mindset, it's not the mindset of God. He wants what's best for us. And when we have the love of God in us, our lives will change from an attitude of "What's in it for me?" to "How can I minister to others?"

LOVE WILL CHANGE YOU INWARDLY

Real love changes the inner person. It changes your motivation, your values, and your beliefs. Why do you love your husband or your wife? Why do you love your mom or dad? Why do you love those who are unlovely? Why do you help those who are in need? Do you ever wonder why? Are you like the man who came to me for counseling not long ago? He was having trouble in his home. He said, "Pastor, my wife treats me terribly, but I'm going to love her because I *have* to love her."

I said, "Where did you get that?"

He said, "Out of the Bible."

I said, "You're wrong! That's not the kind of love you need to have. *Have to* is not the love of God. *Want to* love is the love of God."

We're committed to our parents, our brothers and sisters, our partners for life, and our fellow believers. We're committed to a lost and dying world, to tell them of God's eternal forgiveness. But the real motive in the heart of a true Christian who has God's love within him is, "I want to love them because I've got God's love in my heart!" It's a *want to* love.

Gypsy Smith, a great evangelist in the early twentieth century, went about preaching throughout America, Scotland, and England. Hundreds of thousands heard him, and thousands were converted. He was one of the most powerful preachers ever known. One day a phrenologist (one who studies the skull) came to him and said, "Gypsy, we want to feel your skull and find out the secret of your success." Gypsy said, "Sir, if you're going to find out the secret of my success, you need to go a little lower. You need to go to my heart." You see, God puts love in the heart. His love is the overflowing power of His Spirit dwelling within us. When He controls our lives, love transforms us within.

LOVE WILL CHANGE YOU UPWARDLY

When we are truly converted to Christ, our relationship to God changes and that in turn changes our relationship to our fellow man. When the Holy Spirit puts God's love within us, we radiate that love. This is not the love of Hollywood, of the motion picture or television screen, nor grocery store tabloids. It is the all-powerful love of God.

Where is God? Is He off in the distant cosmos? Is He removed from the needs and problems of people? Not at all. The Bible says that God is the embodiment of love. It is His central character, for God is *love*. How do we love? We love when we're full of God, because when we're full of God, we're full of love.

Paul said, "Though I speak with the tongues of men and of angels, and have not love, I am become as a sounding brass, or a tinkling cymbal" (1 Corinthians 13:1). The next verses go on to say that though I have all the gifts of the Spirit, and I do many marvelous works, and I clothe and feed the poor, if I don't have the love of God within me, I am nothing. In other words, Paul was saying that if we have God in our hearts, we are going to love because God is love. There are three important essentials to the love of God. If these aspects are demonstrated in your life, you can know you have God's love within you and that you have been changed upwardly.

1. God's love is given even when it is undeserved.
The Bible says that God loved us and while we were yet sinners Christ died for us. We didn't deserve God's love, but He gave it to us anyway. He didn't love us because of something we had done for Him, for we had done nothing but reject Him; He loved us because we simply needed His love. God's love is given when it's undeserved. Who among us deserves God's love? None of us. But oh, how we love to receive it.

What about others in our society who don't deserve God's love—those who hate the very things which we cherish to believe? Those who attack us, our faith, even our Lord. Can we ever love them even though they don't deserve it? We can, because that is how God loved us. He loved us when we didn't deserve it, and we can love them with God's love. We who have been loved will love others even when we feel it might be unde-served because God's love lives in and through us.

2. God's love is given even when it's not returned.
In Matthew 5:44, Jesus said, "I say unto you, Love your enemies, bless them that curse you, do good to them that hate you, and pray for them which despite-fully use you, and persecute you." He commanded us to love our enemies. That means we must love those who don't give love in return.

You may have a husband or wife, a son or daughter, a mom or dad that you love dearly. In fact, you love them with all your heart. They know you love them, but they don't give love in return. They never have a kind word or even seem to care. Your heart may ache for them to simply tell you that they love you. But it doesn't happen, so you say, "How can I keep on loving them?" God can help you love them. God gives us love when we don't deserve it, and God shows us how to love others like He loves them, even when that love is not returned.

3. God's love is given without accusation.
The Bible says of Jesus, "He is brought as a lamb to the slaughter, and as a sheep before her shearers is dumb, so he openeth not his mouth" (Isaiah 53:7). When a lamb is brought to slaughter, it will bleat all

the way to the executioner, but once there, becomes silent. That's what the writer had in mind when he talked about Jesus. He came and opened not His mouth. Christ could have avoided the Cross and called ten thousand angels to destroy his crucifiers. But instead, He said, "Father, forgive them." That was the epitome of God's love. In other words, love does not insist on having the final word—love is without accusation. Love doesn't say, "I must have the last word; everything has to go my way or no way at all."

LOVE WILL CHANGE YOU BACKWARDLY

I must admit it sounds a little strange that love will change you backwardly, but the fact is that it is wonderfully true. It changes how you look at your past, regardless of what it has been. Paul said, "Brethren, I count not myself to have apprehended: but this one thing I do, forgetting those things which are behind, and reaching forth unto those things which are before, I press toward the mark for the prize of the high calling of God in Christ Jesus" (Philippians 3:13–14). What was he saying? He was saying that love will change your whole outlook on life. He also said, "Therefore if any man be in Christ, he is a new creature; old things are passed away; behold, all things are become new" (2 Corinthians 5:17).

We have a beautiful song in our hymnal called, "The Love of God." F. M. Lehman wrote the first two verses and the chorus. But the third verse was written by a patient in an asylum for the mentally ill. When the patient died, these words were discovered on the walls of his dark, lonely cell:

Could we with ink the oceans fill,
And were the skies of parchment made;
If ev'ry straw on earth a quill,
And ev'ry man a scribe by trade;
To write the love of God above
Would drain the ocean dry;
Nor could the scroll contain the whole
*Tho' stretched from sky to sky.**

Although he was in the lonely confines of an asylum, he had found that the love of God could reach him even there.

Perhaps you are in your own deep, dark cell today. Perhaps your heart is hardened to the things of God or even to the needs of others. Remember: God loves you. He hasn't given up on you.

Turn to Him and accept His love. Bring your heart to Jesus. He will break it and remold it and make it whole again. A God who loved you enough to let His Son die in your place is worthy of your love. A God who loved you whether or not you loved Him is deserving of your trust. Surrender to Him today and experience a miracle of love that will change your life.

* From "The Love of God" by F. M. Lehman. Copyright 1917. Renewed 1945 by Nazarene Publishing House.

8

YOU CAN BE
SET FREE

■   ■   ■

The Miracle of
Personal Freedom

John 11:40–45

John 11:40–45

40   Jesus saith unto her, Said I not unto thee, that, if thou wouldest believe, thou shouldest see the glory of God?

41   Then they took away the stone from the place where the dead was laid. And Jesus lifted up his eyes, and said, Father, I thank thee that thou hast heard me.

42   And I knew that thou hearest me always: but because of the people which stand by I said it, that they may believe that thou hast sent me.

43   And when he thus had spoken, he cried with a loud voice, Lazarus, come forth.

44   And he that was dead came forth, bound hand and foot with graveclothes; and his face was bound about with a napkin. Jesus saith unto them, Loose him, and let him go.

45   Then many of the Jews which came to Mary, and had seen the things which Jesus did, believed on him.

I had finished speaking at a Bible conference in Delaware, and the host minister had assigned one of the men of his church to drive me back to the Washington Airport for my return flight home.

Wanting to strike up a conversation with him as we rode along, I said, "Tell me about your family."

"Oh," he replied, "I have a wonderful wife and two sweet daughters . . ." There was a slight pause before he continued, "and a sixty-five-year-old son we've adopted."

"A sixty-five-year-old son!" I blurted out in amazement, for the man could not have been over fifty himself. I said, "Tell me about that one."

"Well," he said, "several years ago the police were called to a home in one of our nearby states. It seems there was an older woman who lived in this house all by herself. The neighbors had not seen her come out of the house for some time, so they phoned the police to investigate. When the police arrived, they found the woman in her bedroom, passed out and near death. They called for emergency help and took her to the local hospital. As the police were leaving the house, one of them heard a noise coming from the attic and went to check it out. At the top of the stairs was a heavily bolted door. He unlatched it and there in the darkness of the cold, dusty attic, he found this old man.

His hair and beard hadn't been cut in so long that they reached below his knees. His fingernails were long and stained with age. It appeared he had been kept captive in that attic for many years. They later discovered that the woman had held the man prisoner in her attic for over thirty years. The authorities kept him in a state rehabilitation center for several months, and then my wife and I were allowed to adopt him and bring him into our home to live with us."

After hearing this story that sounded like something out of some incredible storybook, I wanted to know more. "This is absolutely amazing," I said, "how I wish I could have seen that old gentleman while I was here."

"But you did," the man said. "He was the old fellow sitting in the church tonight. You remember, the one near the front with the big smile on his face."

Sure enough, I remembered the man up front who had sat through my entire message that night with an unusually big smile on his face.

As my plane took off for Atlanta, I couldn't get that story out of my mind. Thirty years this man was held captive, and now he was finally free. No wonder he was smiling!

Freedom is something that most Americans take for granted. We have grown up in a country in which we have never known anything other than the blessings of liberty and personal freedom. As a result, our nation has enjoyed the kind of prosperity which naturally comes when people are free to pursue their own interests. However, it is also true that, since we take this freedom for granted, we are often careless about protecting it and passing it on to our next generation.

Anyone living under oppression of any kind will quickly remind you that freedom is one of the greatest blessings of life. Whenever people are free, they can be certain that they have been blessed by God. Each of us should be thankful for our freedom, especially those who know Christ, for ours is a spiritual freedom, and that is the greatest freedom anyone could know.

One of the most dramatic miracles in the ministry of our Lord occurred when He raised His friend, Lazarus, from the dead. The account of this miracle is found in John 11:40–45. Lazarus and his sisters, Mary and Martha, lived in the little town of Bethany, just a few miles south of Jerusalem. Jesus visited with them often and seemed to enjoy their home as a refuge from the pressures of His ministry. On this occasion, a messenger came to Jesus with the news that Lazarus was desperately ill and near death. On hearing this, Jesus waited for two days and then traveled down to Bethany. When He arrived, He found that Lazarus had been dead for four days and had already been buried.

When Mary and Martha discovered that Jesus had come, Martha went to Him and expressed their disappointment at His delay in coming. "Lord, if thou hadst been here, my brother had not died" (John 11:21), she said as she approached the Lord. How difficult those words must have been for Him to hear, for He had loved His friend, Lazarus, and Lazarus' sisters. But soon they all would learn that Jesus' delays are not denials.

Jesus reminded Martha that He was the resurrection and the life, and that those who believed in Him would never die. So Mary joined Martha, and they took the Lord to the place where Lazarus was buried.

When they arrived at the site of the tomb, Jesus commanded the stone to be rolled away. The Bible says

Jesus then lifted up His eyes unto heaven and called upon His Father to hear His prayer and cried with a loud voice, "Lazarus, come forth." The Scripture says, "He that was dead came forth, bound hand and foot with graveclothes; and his face was bound with a napkin. Jesus saith unto them, Loose him, and let him go" (v. 44).

On that day, in Bethany, the ordinary was transformed into the miraculous. This little town would never be the same, for Jesus Christ had come and raised a man from the dead. The news of Lazarus' resurrection spread quickly, and by the time Jesus arrived back in Jerusalem, the people were shouting, "Hosanna," and singing His praises. More importantly, the Bible tells us that the mourners who had gathered in bereavement were transformed from doubt and skepticism to faith in Christ.

What a sight that must have been! As the people stood watching in absolute amazement, Lazarus came forth from the tomb bound in his own graveclothes, much like a walking mummy. As he made his way through the opening of the tomb and stepped into the daylight of life again, the Lord commanded that they loose him and set him free.

There is a revealing aspect to this miracle. While Lazarus had certainly been raised back to life, he was still bound by his old graveclothes. There are many Christians today who have been given life in Christ, but who are still bound by their old ways. Like Lazarus, they, too, have experienced the miracle of resurrection power in their lives, and yet they are not totally free. They are still bound by guilt, fear, old habits, and the mistakes of the past. They know that they have been saved from sin, but they are still struggling with the shame of their past, unable to find their way to the future. Such people are alive in Christ, but are far from enjoying the abundant life of which our Lord spoke so often.

The apostle Paul wrote an entire epistle to the Galatians dealing with this very issue. He addressed Christians who had found true liberty in Jesus, and yet were bound by the restrictions of legalism and keeping the law. The Bible makes it clear that God does not have two plans of salvation: one by faith and one by works. Rather, the Scripture clearly states that we are saved by faith, sanctified by faith, sustained by faith, and that we shall be preserved by faith. This saving faith is a faith that proves itself by our works, to be sure, but those works have nothing to do with securing or maintaining our salvation.

LIFE, LIBERTY, AND HAPPINESS

The American Declaration of Independence states that God has granted certain unalienable rights to all human beings, and that among those are life, liberty, and the pursuit of happiness. While the author may not have had any spiritual connotation in mind, these powerful words certainly reflect a basic biblical truth. Life comes from God, liberty is granted by God, and only in Him can we find true happiness. But even while Americans were enjoying the blessings of liberty in the early days of our nation, there were those black Americans who were still held in the bondage of slavery. Imagine how frustrating it must have been for them to hear other young Americans talk of the blessings of freedom and the privilege of liberty which they could not know. Their plight was not unlike that of those believers today who see the potential for true freedom in Christ, but are enslaved by guilt and spiritual defeat.

Perhaps there is a particular sin which has bound your life and is robbing you of the true blessings of spiritual freedom. You may have fallen into sin or disappointed those you love in some way. Whatever your failure may have been, it is not beyond the reach of God's grace and forgiveness. He is still in the business of forgiving our mistakes, reconciling us unto Himself, and restoring us to service for His cause and purpose.

The following steps can be a guide to discovering the miracle of personal and spiritual freedom in your life. No matter how enslaved or chained you may be to a particular sin, that temptation can be overcome in your life.

1. Total Submission to Christ.

In order to activate God's plan for personal freedom, we must begin with total submission to the person of Jesus Christ. It is that kind of submission that is the evidence of true faith and belief. According to Scripture, believing in Jesus is not merely giving intellectual assent to the fact that He lived or died. Faith in Christ is something far deeper and more significant. It involves the absolute trust and confidence in Him which results in total commitment to Him.

The biblical term for submission comes from the Greek word *huppotasso,* meaning "under authority." This conveys the idea that those who are genuinely committed to someone are also under submission to that person's authority. Such is the case of the commitment of discipleship in following Jesus Christ. As Lord of our lives, Jesus Christ is the ultimate authority to whom we must submit. That submission which we make involves a death to self which allows Him to be in complete control of our lives. No where in the Bible is this illustrated any more powerfully than in the story of Lazarus. He was called forth by Christ and responded in total submission. The result was one of the greatest miracles Jesus ever performed.

We live in a time where there is a great deal of emphasis placed upon self. In fact, ours has been described as the age of selfishness. Advertising and marketing strategies are aimed at urging people to fulfill their selfish urges and desires. Many commercials encourage the viewer to "indulge yourself" or "pamper yourself." Much of this emphasis on self has even crept into our churches, under the guise of accepting one's self or asserting one's self. However, the Bible emphasizes that we are to deny ourselves and to follow Christ. This concept goes against every grain of humanity. But the Scripture makes it clear that it is only in death to self and submission to Christ that we discover the only Person who alone can meet the challenges of life.

If you really want to know the personal and spiritual freedom of God, you will only find it in total commitment to servitude. The great apostle Paul always referred to himself as the "servant of Jesus Christ." In Paul's time, a servant had no rights or privileges of his own. He was in total submission to his master. Even slaves who had been set free could voluntarily be marked for continued service to their master if they so chose. Paul saw himself as that kind of servant. He was one who had been set free by Christ, and yet chose to serve Him continually. It is that attitude of total submission that opens to us the power of spiritual freedom.

2. Total Obedience to Christ.

When Jesus called, "Lazarus, come forth," Lazarus instantly obeyed His command. When he came to life, he did not stay in the tomb, or insist on being released from the graveclothes, nor did he debate the issue. He simply obeyed—immediately!

God will not accept anything less from us than total obedience. It does not matter how many times we come to church, or how much money we give, or how many Bible verses we memorize; God is only moved by our obedience. There is no better example of this than the story of Jonah.

God told Jonah to go to Ninevah and preach the Gospel. Ninevah was the capital of the empire of Assyria, the enemy of the people of Israel. That was the last thing Jonah wanted to do. So he took off in the opposite direction.

Instead of going to Ninevah, Jonah went down to Joppa, a town on the Mediterranean coast, and boarded a boat for Europe. As the boat got further out to sea, God sent a violent storm, and eventually Jonah was thrown overboard to appease God's wrath. He was swallowed by a great fish and spent three days in the depths until, the Bible says, he "prayed to the Lord." Even at the point of his greatest rebellion and the consequences that came from it, Jonah called out unto God for mercy. When the fish spat him up onto dry land, he showed his obedience to God by going to Ninevah and preaching as God had directed him. Like Jonah, once we begin to obey the plan of God, we can expect to see the power of God at work on our behalf to set us free from ourselves so that we might serve Him.

THE POWER OF PERSONAL POTENTIAL

As long as Lazarus was bound in those graveclothes, even though he was alive, he was hopelessly held by the very symbol of death itself. But when Christ raised him from the dead, He also commanded those around him to release him and set him free. These two concepts of resurrection and freedom are inseparable in the plan of God.

God has unlimited potential for your life. But you will never realize your full potential until you experience the freedom that is available in Jesus Christ and you surrender yourself to His will and commit yourself to His purpose. God has a distinctive purpose for each of our lives that no one else can ever fill. That which He has called you to do is as vital a task as any ever undertaken. You are as important to Him as anyone who has ever lived, and through personal faith in Christ, you have a potential to reach beyond what could be reached otherwise.

Your past is no limit to your potential. No matter how much you may have failed God in the past, He still has a potential for you which can be reached in the future. Witness the story of John Newton. Prior to his conversion, he served in the royal navy of England as a slave trader. Later, he became a deserter and turned to piracy. His entire life degenerated into stealing, plundering, and selling slaves.

In spite of the personal sin in his life and the depths of depravity to which he sank, John Newton later came face to face with the claims of Jesus Christ and submitted his life to Him. Over a period of time, God transformed him into a preacher of the grace of God. Later, looking back over his wretched life before meeting Christ and realizing the great grace of God which had been extended to him to bring him to a saving knowledge of Jesus Christ, he wrote these immortal words:

> *Amazing grace, how sweet the sound,*
> *That saved a wretch like me.*
> *I once was lost, but now am found,*
> *Was blind, but now I see.*

In this beloved hymn, Newton emphasized the power of the grace of God moving on behalf of the helpless sinner. He realized that he had been transformed by a power greater than himself and that he had been given a potential which he could never have reached alone.

Don't ever make the mistake of thinking that your life has been wasted. Indeed, you may have wasted a great deal of time living for yourself and chasing the pleasures of this world; but there is always time to make peace with God and begin to serve Him. The whole purpose of the Bible is to communicate to us the fact that we are important to God. That does not mean that God cannot operate the world without us, because He can. What this truth means is that He has not chosen to do so. God has chosen to work through us.

There are two parallel truths that run through Scripture. The Bible makes it clear we are worthless sinners. We have nothing to accredit ourselves to God.

We do not deserve His salvation. But the Bible also makes it clear that we are valuable enough to God that He sent His own Son to die for our sins. That implies that every human soul is valuable to God. If He loved us enough to send His Son to die for us, He certainly loves us enough to lead us unto the wonderful purpose which He has for our lives.

If you are willing to let Him, Jesus Christ will set you free and help you reach that unlimited potential that otherwise could never have been reached.

9

YOU CAN BE MADE CLEAN

■　　　■　　　■

The Miracle of Obedience

2 Kings 5:1-3, 9-14

2 Kings 5:1–3, 9–14

1   Now Naaman, captain of the host of the king of Syria, was a great man with his master, and honorable, because by him the Lord had given deliverance unto Syria: he was also a mighty man in valor, but he was a leper.

2   And the Syrians had gone out by companies, and had brought away captive out of the land of Israel a little maid; and she waited on Naaman's wife.

3   And she said unto her mistress, Would God my lord were with the prophet that is in Samaria! for he would recover him of his leprosy.

. . . .

9   So Naaman came with his horses and with his chariot, and stood at the door of the house of Elisha.

10   And Elisha sent a messenger unto him, saying, Go and wash in Jordan seven times, and thy flesh shall come again to thee, and thou shalt be clean.

11   But Naaman was wroth, and went away, and said, Behold, I thought, He will surely come out to me, and stand, and call on the name of the Lord his God, and strike his hand over the place, and recover the leper.

12   Are not Abana and Pharpar, rivers of Damascus, better than all the waters of Israel? may I not wash in them, and be clean? So he turned and went away in a rage.

13   And his servants came near, and spake unto him, and said, My father, if the prophet had bid thee do some great thing, wouldest thou not have done it? how much rather then, when he saith to thee, Wash, and be clean?

14   Then went he down, and dipped himself seven times in Jordan, according to the saying of the man of God: and his flesh came again like unto the flesh of a little child, and he was clean.

Ever since I was a child, I have been fascinated by the story of Naaman. This man was the captain of the armies of Syria and had reached the pinnacle of success as a warrior. As captain of the hosts of Syria, he was the leader of one of the greatest military forces of his time.

Naaman was such a hero to the people of his nation that he had no doubt become the center of national attention. I can imagine that when the little boys in Syria played soldier, they all wanted to be Naaman. As he would return victorious from his many battles and march through the cities of Syria, no doubt many people would cheer his very presence as he passed by. It is easy to picture him in all of his armor, with his robust chest and his muscles flexing, as he stood with his sword at his side and his feathered helmet tucked under his arm. He was the hero of Syria. In fact, the Bible even calls him a mighty man of valor.

As we read the story in 2 Kings 5:1–14, we learn that in addition to being the "captain of the host of the King of Syria," an "honorable" man, and a "great man" in the eyes of the people, Naaman was also a leper. Somehow this great warrior had contracted the dreadful disease of leprosy which begins at the bone and literally eats away the flesh. Leprosy was so feared in the ancient world that lepers were often made the outcasts of society and people feared to go anywhere near them.

The irony and tragedy in this story is that the man whose military power had inspired others was now inspiring fear because of a dreaded contagious disease. I can imagine how Naaman must have tried to cover himself with his robe or with his armor so that no one would see his disease. But there was no hiding it from himself. When he stood fully armed and ready for battle, underneath the external facade, he knew full well the terrible condition which was quickly spreading within his body.

No one in the known world could cure a leper. When a person contracted this dread disease, he or she was generally doomed for death. Fortunately for Naaman, God had another purpose in mind. An Israelite maiden who had been taken captive by the Syrians and given to Naaman's wife as a servant knew of the ministry of the prophet Elisha, who was in Samaria (or northern Israel) at the time. She told Naaman's wife that if Naaman could only meet Elisha, the prophet would cure him of his leprosy.

Most of us read this story without realizing the animosity that existed at that time between Israel and Syria. For the captain of the Syrian army to cross the border into Israel and to seek the help of a Jewish prophet was unthinkable. However, the Bible tells us that the king of Syria loved Naaman so much that when he heard of this miracle-working prophet, he insisted that Naaman go to Israel and seek him out. The king gave his general a letter to the King of Israel, and Naaman took gold and silver and raiment as gifts to offer the prophet in Israel.

What a stir it must have caused, as Naaman crossed

the border in his military chariot with his great band of soldiers. When the king of Israel learned that Naaman had come to Israel to be healed of his leprosy, he became hysterical in fear and tore his clothes as a sign of his helplessness. "Am I God?" he said, "to kill and make alive, that this man doth send unto me to recover a man of his leprosy?" (v. 7).

When Elisha the prophet heard of this, he sent word for Naaman to come to his house, and there God would prove to him that there was a true prophet in Israel. What a scene that must have been as this mighty military captain pulled his chariot to a halt in front of the humble abode of the prophet of God. Picture with me as Naaman commands one of his soldiers to beckon the prophet out to stand before him. Dismounting his steed, his armor clangs as he walks across the wooden porch and bangs upon the door with a shout, "You in there, come out and stand before Naaman, captain of the hosts of Syria!"

However, Elisha did not go out to meet Naaman. Instead he sent his servant out to deliver his message to the Syrian captain. The message was simple, yet would bear within it many complexities for Naaman's heart. It was, "Go and wash in Jordan seven times, and thy flesh shall come again to thee, and thou shalt be clean" (v. 10).

As Naaman listened to the prophet's demands, his face must have reddened, his veins swelling within his neck in anger. He had expected something far greater from the prophet. He had thought that certainly this man of Israel would have come out and waved his hand over the place and called upon his God to heal the leper, but instead, to be commanded to go and wash in the river Jordan was an insult too great to take. The Scripture says, "so he turned and went away in a rage" (v. 12).

Naaman had servants who loved him, and because of their great love, they went crying after him. "My father," they said, "if the prophet had bid thee do some great thing, wouldest thou not have done it? How much rather then, when he saith to thee, Wash, and be clean?" (v. 13). So Naaman went down to Jordan, dipped seven times in perfect obedience to the prophet's command, and his flesh came unto him again, as perfect as a little child's.

What joy filled Naaman's heart as he returned to Elisha and confessed, "Now I know that there is no God in all the earth but in Israel" (v. 15).

Naaman's story demonstrates the powerful fact that it is simple obedience which brings the greatest miracle-working power of God into our lives. While Naaman certainly experienced an incredible miracle of healing, he also experienced an even deeper miracle of obedience in his life. His story also serves to remind us that God uses simple means to accomplish great things. Nothing that the prophet did called attention to himself or his abilities. All that transpired pointed Naaman to the God who alone could meet his needs.

DEALING WITH OUR POINT OF PRIDE

God's demands for obedience are often aimed at our greatest points of pride. The prophet initially made Naaman angry because he undermined his pride in the power of his position. The Scripture makes it clear that Naaman obviously thought that because of his great position of authority and his successful military reputation, the prophet would go out of his way to put on an extra special demonstration on his behalf. What a shock it must have been when the prophet did not even meet with him personally but instead sent a servant to ask him to do something that seemed to Naaman utterly humiliating.

Why was Naaman so angry? Because God had offended his point of pride. The Jordan River served as the border between Syria and Israel at that time, and Naaman had undoubtedly crossed it on many occasions. How was he to believe that simply dipping himself in it seven times would bring about any kind of healing? Yet it was only in the breaking of his pride that he finally found the God of Israel who was the real source of power which he sought.

When God calls us to obedience, His demands will inevitably offend our pride and bring us to a point of humility. The reason for that is that God understands exactly what is standing between us and Him. He knows that our point of pride is that which we are least willing to surrender to Him. Whenever we tell God, "I will do anything you want me to do, except *this one thing,*" that thing represents our point of pride. Whenever we try to leave God out of a certain area of our lives, we can be sure that He will deal with that area. This does not mean that God wants to take things away from us that are valuable to us, but that He wants us to yield those things to His will for our lives.

God is not a robber of joy, but a giver of joy. God is not One who delights to take things away from us, but rather, is the One who delights to give things to us. However, when we become so satisfied with His gifts that we forget who the Giver really is, then He will always do whatever is necessary to get our attention.

Most of us get angry when our pride is struck. But it is only in the breaking of that pride that we ever experience the kind of spiritual brokenness that leads to true greatness. The Bible reminds us that "pride goes before destruction," and that God "resists the proud." That is exactly what was happening in Naaman's life, and it is exactly what happens in our lives as well.

Greek mythology tells of two wrestlers who participated in the Olympic games. One was older and greatly experienced in his craft, while the other was young and inexperienced. Often these two would wrestle before the crowds, and always the older man would win. Through the years the young wrestler built up a great hatred in his heart toward his foe because of the many humiliating defeats at his hands. Time and again his pride was offended. Finally, the older wrestler died and a bronze statue of him was erected in the arena in memory of his many victories. One night the young man, whose heart was filled with hatred, went to the statue. Climbing up, he grabbed it around the waist and shouted, "Now, my great foe, I'll show you who is the greatest. Beat me now, if you can!" As he struggled, trying to topple it, he fell to the ground and the statue fell on top of him crushing him to death. His pride had destroyed his very life.

It has been said that pride is the anesthetic that dulls the pain of stupidity. Pride is an abomination to God. It causes us to do some of the most foolish and selfish things that human beings could ever attempt. Whatever the point of pride is in your life, God will deal with it sooner or later. When He does, do not resist His working in your life, but learn the lesson of obedience to Him and His will.

St. Augustine stated many years ago that there are

only two kinds of people in this world. There is the person who loves himself so much that he brings contempt to God. And there is the person who loves God so much that he brings contempt to himself. One of the greatest problems of modern man is that of self love. Ours is a selfish love and self-centered society in which people tend to put self before God and others.

Learn the spirit of humility. The word *humility* comes from the Latin root *humus* which means "ground." You must come down to the ground before God will ever raise you up.

HUMBLE MEANS OFTEN BRING THE GREATEST RESULTS

The story of Elisha and Naaman also reminds us that God often uses humble means to bring about His greatest results. Two of the greatest evangelists America has ever known were led to Christ by simple people whose names have been all but forgotten. Billy Sunday was a professional baseball player of some notoriety in Chicago, but his life had fallen apart and he found himself wandering into a rescue mission, desperately in search of God. That night someone preached, Sunday responded to the invitation, and someone else led him to Christ. Billy Sunday went on to a successful career as an evangelist, but we have long forgotten the names of those who pointed the way. Dwight L. Moody, another great evangelist, was a shoe clerk who was led to Christ by a relatively obscure shoe salesman. In time, God used Moody to shake two continents for Christ. Today nearly every Christian knows the name of D. L. Moody, but who remembers the Boston shoe salesman who brought him to Christ?

God often uses seemingly insignificant people and things of this world to accomplish His purposes. Rather than choose the powerful and mighty people, God has often chosen those in relative obscurity to fulfill His will. God may be determined to use the smallest and humblest of people because He knows that men are prone to glorify themselves, rather than Him. We have all been guilty of glorifying the servants of God, rather than the God whom they serve. Even preachers of the gospel are susceptible to failure because they are fallible human beings. When someone fails, your faith need not be shaken unless you have placed your faith in God's servants, rather than in God Himself.

God used insignificant and unnamed servants in the story of Naaman to accomplish His purposes. We are not told the name of the Israelite servant girl who urged Naaman to go to Samaria, or the name of Elisha's servant who was sent to deliver the prophet's message to Naaman, or the name of Naaman's servants who urged him to obey the request of the prophet. While it is clear in this story that God uses those who love us to encourage us to obey, it is also clear that the ultimate issues of life are between us and God Himself. Even the prophet Elisha, through whom the miracle-working message was delivered, refused to take any reward or gift from Naaman, so that he might make it clear that he had not done any of this for personal gain. While the Bible certainly teaches that the laborer is worthy of his hire and that God's servants ought to be cared for by God's people, nowhere does the Bible validate the idea of trying to acquire personal gain from the ministry.

To be first is to be last, Jesus taught us, and to be last is to be first!

GOD HAS NO INTERMISSIONS

Once Naaman was willing to obey God's command, the Lord Himself set in motion His miracle-working process. As soon as Naaman dipped into the Jordan for the seventh time and came up out of the water, he was instantly cured. In the same way, the only thing that it takes to move God on our behalf is simple obedience to His Word.

When we obey, God moves. This does not make God our puppet; we cannot make Him move on our behalf unless He chooses to do so. However, when He clearly commands us to do something and we obey that command, we can expect immediate results. Naaman learned that there was no intermission (that is, no lapsed time) between his obedience and God's miraculous working. His skin immediately became like that of a child. I'm sure that Naaman would have been satisfied to have had middle-aged skin as long as the leprosy was gone. However, God not only cured Naaman of his immediate need, He restored him physically beyond anything that he could have imagined.

When God cleanses us, He does it thoroughly and completely. In Naaman's case it was a physical cleansing, but this principle is also true for those who need spiritual cleansing. When we come by faith to the foot of the Cross, God wipes away every impurity and makes us whole by the cleansing power of the blood of Jesus Christ. It does not matter how great your sins may have been, nor how unclean you may feel, the grace of God is greater than all our sin and His miraculous power to wash us clean is all that we need to prepare us for heaven.

A retired military chaplain once told of an incident that occurred to him while serving on the battlefield in World War II. He was walking through a twisted maze of dead and wounded bodies when he heard the groans of a dying young man. As he bent over the battered and bloody frame of the young soldier, he said, "Young man, is there anything that I can do for you?"

The young soldier looked up through dying eyes and said, "I don't need anyone to do something for me, but I need somebody to undo all the things that I have done before it's too late."

That is exactly who God is. He is the One who is able to "undo" all our mistakes of the past. He is there for rescuing souls, forgiving sins, and cleansing lives. It is never too late to come to Him. The miracle of obedience can make you clean.

10

TAKING ADVANTAGE
OF THE MOMENT

■   ■   ■

The Miracle of Courage

Mark 10:46–52

Mark 10:46–52

46 And they came to Jericho: and as he went out of Jericho with his disciples and a great number of people, blind Bartimeus, the son of Timeus, sat by the highway side begging.

47 And when he heard that it was Jesus of Nazareth, he began to cry out, and say, Jesus, thou Son of David, have mercy on me.

48 And many charged him that he should hold his peace: but he cried the more a great deal, Thou Son of David, have mercy on me.

49 And Jesus stood still, and commanded him to be called. And they call the blind man, saying unto him, Be of good comfort, rise; he calleth thee.

50 And he, casting away his garment, rose, and came to Jesus.

51 And Jesus answered and said unto him, What wilt thou that I should do unto thee? The blind man said unto him, Lord, that I might receive my sight.

52 And Jesus said unto him, Go thy way; thy faith hath made thee whole. And immediately he received his sight, and followed Jesus in the way.

Courage is something which most of us lack—especially in the face of opposition. It is easy to talk about having courage, but it is another matter altogether to have it at the moment we need it. Sometimes we lack the courage to admit our weaknesses and call out for help. I can recall as a child being afraid in the dark, and yet, also being too afraid to call out to anyone to help me. At other times we lack the courage to take hold of some once-in-a-lifetime opportunity that is set before us, and when the opportunity comes, we sit in silence, and live the rest of our lives wondering why we didn't seize the moment of chance when we had it.

There is a beautiful story told from the life of Christ about a man named Bartimeus. He was blind and desperately in need of the miracle touch of Christ. The Scripture tells us that as Jesus was leaving Jericho, He was followed by a great crowd of people. Bartimeus, who was sitting by the roadside begging, heard from the crowd that Jesus of Nazareth was passing by.

Realizing that this moment was his one chance to be healed, Bartimeus cried out for Jesus to help him. Those surrounding the beggar said, "Bartimeus, hold your peace—keep quiet and don't bother Jesus." Ignoring them, he cried out all the louder and more fervently for help. Hearing his cry, Jesus stood still and commanded that they bring the blind man unto Him. The courage of this poor blind beggar should challenge our own hearts. At the moment of his greatest need, he was unwilling to sit quietly by and let this opportunity escape him. Instead, he cried out until he attracted Jesus' attention and the Savior stopped and responded.

This account is found in Mark 10:46–52. It is a wonderful illustration of Christ's miracle-working ministry. When our Lord asked the blind man what he wanted, Bartimeus responded that he desired to receive his sight. Jesus then said, "Go thy way; thy faith hath made thee whole." The Scripture says Bartimeus *immediately* received his sight and followed after Jesus.

While you may acknowledge that this is a marvelous story, you may also wonder how it applies to your own life. The same principles which were at work in the transformation of Bartimeus are still at work in our lives today. Perhaps you are struggling with a deep personal problem even at this very moment. You may be so overwhelmed by that problem that you are losing the courage to even face life itself! Remember, God's love and miracle-working power are just as available today as they were during the time when our Savior walked upon this earth. What happened to Bartimeus in that time is no different from what can happen to you today.

God is still in the miracle-working business. All that is needed are the proper ingredients of righteousness and the catalyst of courage to set into motion the power of God for us all.

ACKNOWLEDGE YOUR NEED

One of the most amazing aspects of the account of Jesus' healing of Bartimeus is the fact that our Lord responded to his plea by asking him what he wanted. It had to be obvious to Christ that the man was blind and that his request would be related to that particular need. However, Jesus made Bartimeus express that need personally.

As strange as it sounds, many people never receive the help they need because they lack the courage to admit their need. In the account of Bartimeus, there were really two miracles: one of physical healing and one of spiritual healing.

Many people are spiritually blind and do not know it. The great irony of life is that while physical blindness is obvious to everyone, spiritual blindness is not. Many of those who are spiritually blind try to convince themselves that their view of life is adequate and sufficient. But the Bible says that a person is spiritually blind when he has never seen what Jesus Christ can do for him. 2 Corinthians 4:4 says, "The gods of this world hath blinded the minds of them which believe not." When you cannot see who Christ is and what He has done for you, then Satan has blinded you to the truth of what life is really all about. Satan is the most miserable character in the universe. He is a loser who has already been defeated by the powerful atonement of Christ on the cross.

Have you ever observed a losing ball team? They usually are filled with complaints and excuses. Their heads are hung down and their countenance has fallen in such a way that their misery is obvious to everyone.

That is how Satan is! He is a miserable, defeated loser. Unfortunately, in his misery, he is also out to cheat you out of the joy and hope which God has provided for you. He will actually attempt to tell you that the Christian life is the most miserable thing that you could ever experience. If you believe him, you will be blind to the truth of what life is really all about.

I remember hearing a story not long ago about two boys from the country who were riding on a train for the very first time. As they sat in their seats, and looked out of the windows, they were filled with amazement. The train was zooming and the scenery was flashing past their eyes as they gazed in wonder. Eventually a porter came through the car selling bananas. Each boy bought one and about the time the first boy took a bite of his banana, the train went into a deep, dark, long tunnel. As the two boys sat in stunned silence, one said to the other, "John, have you eaten your banana yet?" "No, why?" his friend responded. "Well, don't do it, cause if you do, it'll make you blind as a bat!"

We can laugh at this ridiculous story, but the lies of the Devil make just as little sense. He wants to blind us to the real cause and effect relationships of life. He is especially delighted when we are blind to God's power which is available to us and His provisions to meet our needs. Remember, the first step in finding the miracle you need is to have the courage to acknowledge your need in the first place.

ASK GOD FOR HELP

When Bartimeus heard that Jesus was passing by, he immediately began to cry out. He did not merely sit there and consider his options. He did something about it! He cried out as loudly as he could, in spite of the throng of people around him. While the beggar's shouts may have been an embarrassment to his friends, desperate people know no embarrassment. Bartimeus not only cried out persistently, but he also called out, "Jesus, thou Son of David." Such a reference was an acknowledgment of the claim of Jesus to be the Messiah, the descendant of David. Thus, Bartimeus' appeal was directly made to the authority of Christ Himself. It was that request which stopped our Lord in His tracks.

You may be facing a crisis in your own life at this very moment. If you are, do not hesitate to call upon God for help. In the face of our greatest calamities, God's great grace can overcome any obstacle that we face. In such times of need, we must learn to pray with a sincerity and fervency that reaches from the very depth of our being. When you become desperate enough to seek God with all your heart, realizing that He is the only solution to your problems, then you will receive courage to trust God for a miracle in your behalf.

BE READY TO RESPOND

When Jesus responded to Bartimeus' plea, He called him to Himself. The Scripture tells us that the beggar cast away his garment, rose and came to Jesus. Notice that Christ did not come to the beggar, but rather that He called the beggar to come to Him. Virtually every miracle that God does on our behalf demands a response from us personally.

Bartimeus had probably been sitting by the wayside

of that dusty road for years. His garment was undoubtedly filthy, and the beggar himself was anything but an example of cleanliness. At the same time, that garment was all the security that Bartimeus had with which to clothe himself. But in this moment of greatest possibility, he was willing to throw it aside, parting with his false and unclean garment of security in order to come into the presence of the Lord.

Why is it people think they can come to God, clutching the rags of their own sinful lifestyles, and expect God to work in their behalf? If there is one great theme of the Bible it is that God is holy. He is separated from sin and can have no fellowship with it. The first step toward coming to God is confessing our sins, casting off the filthy garments of transgressions, and then approaching His throne of grace. He will receive us in no other way: only after we have, through His forgiveness, cleaned up our hearts.

Louis XIV of France was one of the greatest kings who ever lived. He was also apparently one of the filthiest men who ever lived. It is said that he only took a bath once a year, and that he only did that because his doctors insisted upon it. They literally held him down and bathed him annually. In fact, he was so unwilling to bathe on a regular basis that he eventually commissioned a chemist to develop a substance that he could put on his body so that he would never have to take another bath. The chemist eventually developed that substance from the pollen of flowers and presented it to the king. Every morning Louis XIV doused himself with this liquid so that people could stand to be in his presence. That substance was known as perfume.

We can douse ourselves with the perfume of good

works and noble efforts for an entire lifetime and never experience the cleansing grace of God. We can attend church, give money to the Sunday school, and even tell others about Jesus Christ without ever coming to personal faith in Him ourselves.

The Bible never teaches us that God's acceptance is dependent upon our good works. If we had to cleanse ourselves from sin, we would all perish. However, the Bible does tell us that God has made cleansing possible to all who will come to Him by faith. The prophet Isaiah said, "Come now, let us reason together, saith the Lord: though your sins be as scarlet, they shall be as white as snow; though they be red like crimson, they shall be as wool" (Isaiah 1:18). The Psalmist said, "As far as the east is from the west, so far hath he removed our transgressions from us" (Psalm 103:12). The apostle Peter said, "Repent ye therefore, and be converted, that your sins may be blotted out" (Acts 3:19). The apostle John put it this way, "If we confess our sins, he is faithful and just to forgive us our sins, and to cleanse us from all unrighteousness" (1 John 1:9).

What greater promises could anyone have? God has clearly stated in His Word that He will make every provision to cleanse us from our sins, blot them out, remove them, wash them, and forgive them. There is nothing that we can do to save ourselves; He has done it all. In light of that, the only response we need to make is to cast ourselves upon His grace and to trust His wonderful provision as adequate payment for our sins, believing the promise of His invitation is for us personally. It is no wonder that the hymn writer said,

What can wash away my sins?
Nothing but the blood of Jesus.

ACCEPT GOD'S OFFER

There must also come a point in our lives when we must have the courage to accept God's provision for our needs. Had Bartimeus remained silent, there would not have been any solution to the problem of his blindness. But, in his moment of opportunity, he received the miracle of courage to cry out by faith for that which only Christ could do for him. Shouting above the din of the crowd, Bartimeus caught the attention of the Savior, and Jesus called him to come to Him. When Bartimeus requested the restoration of his sight, Jesus simply said, "Go thy way; thy faith hath made thee whole" (Mark 10:52). The Bible tells us that the beggar immediately "received his sight, and followed Jesus in the way." This literally means that he became a follower of Jesus Christ. The term *the way* was the early phrase by which Christianity was known. The concept comes from the Old Testament term *hallachah* which means "a way of life." In other words, from that point on, Jesus Christ became the way of life for Bartimeus. Hence, Jesus' early disciples were known as followers of "the way."

From that day on, Bartimeus was known to one and all as the man whom Jesus healed. He would be known as one who walked with Christ Himself. And just as He passed by Bartimeus so many years ago, Christ is passing your way today. Take advantage of the moment and call out to Him from the depth of your need. Just as He met the need of that blind beggar, He will meet your needs as well.

I have a plaque that someone gave me several years ago. Under the title "COURAGE" are these words by an unnamed writer who understood the true definition of courage.

Why is it that most men's lives are controlled by small and petty circumstances? I am saddened as I watch people lose the good and great things that are within their reach and could be theirs with "but a little act of courage!"

Courage is the most beautiful of all human expressions. Courage as I see it is, "an act in the face of fear." We only need courage when we are afraid, which means that we need courage almost all of the time, because we are afraid of something all of the time.

I have discovered that fear becomes a coward when faced with but a small act of courage, and further, that the muscle of courage will grow strong with continued use.

My advice to myself is, "do those things which you fear, and keep doing them until you are no longer afraid, and then you will have become the master of your fate."

I have studied the deeds of men both great and small, and I have studied those men who are great and small. In this study there appear to be many differences. All of the differences which count have, at their base, one single thing—courage.

Courage is that one ingredient which separates the weak from the strong, the successful from the weak, the great from the average. All the things you desire in life have one common handle, which is made for the hand of the person with courage. To be afraid is to be alive. To act in the face of fear is to be a man.

11

LAYING HOLD OF YOUR PROMISE

■ ■ ■

The Miracle of Fulfillment

Joshua 3:1–7

Joshua 3:1–7

1 And Joshua rose early in the morning; and they removed from Shittim, and came to Jordan, he and all the children of Israel, and lodged there before they passed over.

2 And it came to pass after three days, that the officers went through the host;

3 And they commanded the people, saying, When ye see the ark of the covenant of the Lord your God, and the priests the Levites bearing it, then ye shall remove from your place, and go after it.

4 Yet there shall be a space between you and it, about two thousand cubits by measure: come not near unto it, that ye may know the way by which ye must go: for ye have not passed this way heretofore.

5 And Joshua said unto the people, Sanctify yourselves: for to-morrow the Lord will do wonders among you.

6 And Joshua spake unto the priests, saying, Take up the ark of the covenant, and pass over before the people. And they took up the ark of the covenant, and went before the people.

7 And the Lord said unto Joshua, This day will I begin to magnify thee in the sight of all Israel, that they may know that, as I was with Moses, so I will be with thee.

When I was a boy, I tended to believe almost everything people told me. If someone made me a promise, I just assumed that they meant to keep it. As I grew older, I learned that not every promise could be trusted nor taken seriously. Someone might casually promise me something, but unfortunately they had little intention of ever actually doing it. Just recently I asked a repairman who had broken a promise why he had done it. His reply was, "Well, I guess I'm just human." He was right. We humans have a way of breaking promises and letting folks down.

Unlike human promises, however, the promises of God can be trusted with absolute confidence. You and I need never worry about whether or not God intends to fulfill His promises. The apostle Peter said, "The Lord is not slack concerning His promise" (2 Peter 3:9). Peter was right. Again and again the Bible assures us that what God said He would do, He will do!

Whenever I think of biblical promises, I am reminded of the story found in the early chapters of the book of Joshua where God promised to make Joshua victorious and give the land of Canaan to the people of Israel.

No people ever faced greater obstacles than did the Israelites in the Old Testament. They had been in bondage in Egypt for some four hundred years. Even after their miraculous crossing of the Red Sea and their deliverance from the Egyptians, they had spent an additional forty years wandering in the wilderness of Sinai. For all those years they had tenaciously clung to the promise that God had made to their forefather, Abraham, that He would give the land of Canaan to his descendants. They knew that this promised land "flowed with milk and honey," and that it was all that they had ever heard it was and more than enough to meet their needs.

As the children of Israel followed Joshua through the wilderness to the outskirts of the Promised Land, they faced two immediate obstacles. First, the Jordan River, which served as a natural boundary between them and the land of Canaan, was flooded over its banks as they approached it. Second, the mighty Canaanites and several other tribes of people occupied the various parts of that land, and they were not about to relinquish it without a fight. These obstacles, however, were insignificant in light of the promise of God. The Lord had said unto Joshua, "Every place that the sole of your foot shall tread upon, that have I given unto you" (Joshua 1:3). God had named the borders of Israel which would extend from Lebanon in the north to Egypt in the south, and from the Mediterranean on the west to the Euphrates River on the east. He further promised Joshua that none of the people of the land of Canaan would be able to stand before him if he would meditate on His Word day and night and obey all that He commanded him to do. With the promise of God before him and the power of God within him, Joshua marched forward in victorious obedience.

PROMISES, PLANS, AND POWER

God's promises are always made in accordance with His plans for us. And it is only to the degree that we lay hold of His promises that we will see the plan and purpose of God unfolded in our lives. It is also to this degree that we will see the power of God at work on our behalf. These three P's all work simultaneously: promises, plans, and power. As we believe the promises of God, and act upon the plan of God, we will always experience the power of God in our lives.

In order to reinforce His promise to Joshua, the Lord commanded him to bring the people of Israel to the banks of the Jordan River. When they arrived, they found the river overflowing its banks, making it all but impossible to cross.

In order to focus their attention on God Himself, the Lord told Joshua to command the priests to carry the ark of the covenant into the Jordan River. (The ark of the covenant was the place where the blood of sacrifice was applied to the mercy seat and where the glory of God resided among the Israelites. In essence, the ark of the covenant symbolized God's power and presence with His people.) The Scriptures tell us that the priests carried the ark into the river and as the soles of their feet rested in the waters of the Jordan, the Israelites were able to cross over on dry land!

Just as Moses had miraculously led the children of Israel across the Red Sea at the beginning of their journey, now Joshua led them miraculously across the Jordan River at the end of their journey. In all, it had been a journey of faith. For some, it had been a very difficult time in which hard lessons had to be learned. In fact, a whole generation had been lost in the wilderness. But now the people were ready to believe God and to obey His word. As they followed the ark of the covenant across the Jordan River on dry land they knew that they could trust the promises of God because they were beginning to see them fulfilled. A covenant is an agreement or a promise. The ark of the covenant also represented the fulfillment of God's promises to His people. As the Israelites watched the ark of promise being taken across the river, their own faith in the promises of God was being strengthened.

KEEP YOUR EYES ON THE GOAL

There are over thirty thousand promises in the Word of God. Once we begin to understand the nature of these promises and our own potential to see them fulfilled, we will begin to mature in our walk of faith. These promises are designed to activate our confidence in God. Once we realize that God has made abundant personal promises to us, our minds will be enlightened, and we will catch sight of what God is doing in this world. At that point, nothing else will matter. All the things that we have put before the Lordship of Christ will fade into insignificance. Once you taste of the great things that God has for you, you will never want to go back to a mediocre spiritual walk with Him.

Once we catch sight of the promise, we must continually keep the promise in view. As the Israelites focused on the ark of the covenant, and thereby on the promises of God, they remained transfixed until they had safely crossed the river. One of the truths which is taught in the Old Testament is that our focus and attention must be on God and not on man. That is why the priests carried the ark into the water first, so the people could see it before them. That is also why the people obediently and confidently followed. As we keep the promises of God continually before us, we will be motivated to activate those promises in our lives.

Personal worth and value are not things which can merely be attributed to our income, possessions, or status in life. In the ultimate sense, our own personal worth can only be determined in light of the death of Christ for us. If God were willing to do that for us, then how much more can we trust Him with every detail of our lives? Just as the Israelites focused straight ahead on the ark of the covenant as the waters of the Jordan divided, so must we do the same. When the storms of life billow against you, keep your eyes on the Promiser and not the circumstances. Remember, being a Christian will not make you immune to the problems of life. But the exciting news for believers is that God's promises are greater than our problems.

When the problems become the toughest, God's promises become the dearest. It is only in light of the great tragedies and necessities of life that we really begin to fully understand and appreciate the depth and significance of God's promises to us. As we begin to claim those promises and see them beautifully fulfilled in our lives, we understand that God is the One who alone can bring us through the difficulties and set us on solid ground.

MAKING PROMISES BECOME REALITY

In the book of Joshua, chapter 3, the Bible presents three prerequisites for seeing God's promises come to pass.

1. A Clean Heart.

As Joshua prepared the children of Israel for their miraculous crossing, He told them to "sanctify yourselves" (v. 5). He was calling upon them to repent and cleanse their hearts in order that they might serve the Lord. There are many promises of God recorded in Scripture which will never be fulfilled in our lives if we merely attempt to claim them in the arm of the flesh. We cannot expect God to move miraculously on our behalf to fulfill His promises to us unless our hearts are right with Him.

Spiritual heart surgery takes diligence and discipline. It involves cutting away that which is displeasing to God and replacing it with that which pleases Him. In many ways the Christian life involves the same kind of diligence and precise care as medical heart surgery. Only when our hearts are right with God can we expect the fulfillment of His promises in our lives.

2. A Focused Mind.

Not only were the Israelites to properly prepare themselves spiritually by the means of spiritual sanctification, but they were also to focus their attention on the ark of the covenant, and thereby, on God Himself. Leaving behind their negative traditions, they focused on the future. When Joshua told the people of Israel to follow the priests into the Jordan River, they could have easily questioned the wisdom of such a command. But, by this time, the Israelites had learned that obedience was certainly a better option than disobedience. When the priests stepped forward, the people readily followed after them.

Most of us have difficulty attempting great things for God because we are so unwilling to break with tradition. If it hasn't been done before, we are reluctant to be the first ones to take a step of faith in a new direction. Although some traditions can be healthy and need to be followed, others can destroy vision and cause us to come up on the short end of what God has for us.

I remember hearing the story of a man who walked into the kitchen one day when his wife was preparing to bake a ham. He had noticed it was always her tradition to cut off the end of the ham before she baked it. He had wondered why she did it that way, so he asked her. "Honey," he said, "why do you always cut off the end of the ham before you cook it?" "I don't know," she replied, "it's just the way my mother always did it." Now, he thought to himself, when her mother comes for Thanksgiving, I'll ask her why it's done that way. When Thanksgiving came, the man asked his mother-in-law, "Mother, why do you always cut off the end of the ham before you cook it?" "Oh," she said, "I really don't know for sure, it's just the way my mother taught me to do it." Now he was really exasperated! "Well," he thought, "when Grandmother comes for Christmas I'll ask her why she does it that way." So Christmas finally came and the man asked his grandmother-in-law, "Grandmother, when you cook hams, why do you always cut off the ends before you cook them?" "Oh, son," she replied, "I always cut off the ends because I have a short pan!"

I never hear that story without thinking about the joys that have been missed, the gifts of God that we have all been robbed of, and the many who could have been, but were not, won to Christ, because so many Christians have bound themselves down to the traditions of others who had spiritually short pans.

Whatever you attempt to do for God, keep your eyes focused upon Him and GET A BIG PAN!

What the Israelites had come to understand under Joshua's leadership was that God was a big God and able to fulfill His promises then and there. Remember, these were not the Israelites who had crossed the Red Sea, for most of them had died in the wilderness. For the most part, this was a younger generation who had been born in that wilderness experience and who had heard the stories their parents had told them of God's miraculous deliverance forty years earlier.

It is our tendency today to concentrate on the stories of spiritual revival and awakening in the past. We often hear accounts of the great movings of God in the days of Whitfield, Wesley, and Edwards. Or we hear about the revivals of Finney, Moody, and Sunday. But rarely do we talk about what God is doing today! The truth is that the same miracle-working power that was available to believers in generations gone by is available to us today. We, too, can expect by faith to see God at work on our behalf when our hearts are right and our minds are focused on Him.

3. Unquestioned Obedience.

Joshua told the priests to put the ark of the covenant upon their shoulders and to step into the waters of the Jordan River. Then he told the people to follow them across the river to the other side. The Israelites did not stand there and argue with Joshua or try to present an alternative plan. They had no minority report to deliver and no votes to take. They moved ahead with unquestioned obedience.

Unfortunately, we rarely see that kind of obedience demonstrated in God's people today. We tend to obey only when we are virtually forced to and even then it is usually without the right heart attitude. Too often we are like the little boy who was standing on the chair at the dinner table. When his mother insisted that he sit down, he refused to do so. Therefore, she spanked him and made him sit in the chair. As he was sitting there, she remarked, "Now, don't you feel better sitting down?"

"No!" he insisted, "I'm still standing on the inside!"

Such half-hearted obedience will never bring the blessing of God upon your life. If you really want to see the promises of God fulfilled in your life, surrender to Him in unquestioned obedience and you will experience His unlimited power in your life.

EXPECT THE MIRACLE!

There is one other factor which is necessary in order to see God's promises fulfilled for us. That is: we must *expect* those promises to be fulfilled. That is where the elements of faith and confidence enter in. It is one thing to know what God's promises are, and to even believe that they could be fulfilled; but it is another thing to *expect* them to be fulfilled. It is at this point that we actualize our faith. Believers often take the attitude that God might fulfill His promises to others, but not to them. We can even become excited when someone else has an answered prayer, but we rarely expect such answers to our own personal needs. True faith believes God's promises and trusts Him for their fulfillment.

If Joshua and the people of Israel had not expected God to fulfill His word, they would have turned back into the wilderness, even as their forefathers did. Instead, they realized that they were in a position to trust God as they never had before and put Him to the test. And it was a difficult position, to say the least: crossing the swollen River Jordan with hostile enemy forces waiting for them on the other side. Yet, it was exactly where they needed to be—where they were absolutely forced to expect God to deliver them. It is in such moments of faith that God is pleased to bless us and show His faithfulness in our deliverance.

You may not have such rivers to cross in your own life today. But one day you'll find yourself, as we all do, in some situation in which only God can help you. When that day comes, remember that the God who delivered the people of Israel can deliver you as well. His help, love, and power are just as real today as ever. Trust Him, claim His promises, and you will not be disappointed.

Here then is a wonderful formula for seeing the fulfillment of God's promises. Put it to the test. I think you will find it greatly rewarding.

HOW TO HAVE GOD'S PROMISES FULFILLED

God's Word on the Matter
+ A Clean Heart
+ A Focused Mind
+ Unquestioned Obedience
= Promises Fulfilled.

12

SURVIVING THROUGH THE STORMS

■ ■ ■

The Miracle of Endurance

Acts 27:18–25

18   And we being exceedingly tossed with a tempest, the next day they lightened the ship;

19   And the third day we cast out with our own hands the tackling of the ship.

20   And when neither sun nor stars in many days appeared, and no small tempest lay on us, all hope that we should be saved was then taken away.

21   But after long abstinence, Paul stood forth in the midst of them, and said, Sirs, ye should have hearkened unto me, and not have loosed from Crete, and to have gained this harm and loss.

22   And now I exhort you to be of good cheer: for there shall be no loss of any man's life among you, but of the ship.

23   For there stood by me this night the angel of God, whose I am, and whom I serve,

24   Saying, Fear not, Paul; thou must be brought before Caesar: and, lo, God hath given thee all them that sail with thee.

25   Wherefore, sirs, be of good cheer: for I believe God, that it shall be even as it was told me.

It is impossible to get through life without facing a few stormy situations.

Columnist Ann Landers once wrote, "If I were asked to give what I consider the single most useful bit of advice for all humanity, it would be this: Expect trouble as an inevitable part of life, and when it comes, hold your head high, look it squarely in the eye, and say, 'I will be bigger than you. You cannot defeat me!'" That's pretty good advice.

From the very beginning of the apostle Paul's Christian experience, it seems that he was always in trouble. You may recall the time that he had to be lowered over the wall in a basket in order to escape those who were angry at his preaching. There were other incidents where he was beaten, imprisoned, and on one occasion, stoned and left for dead. Finally, when Paul was nearing the end of his third missionary journey, he was imprisoned in Israel at the Roman fortress at Caesarea, and from there sent by ship to stand trial before Caesar himself. In Acts 27, the Bible recounts the story of Paul's fateful journey across the Mediterranean Sea. Chained to a Roman centurion, Paul rode prisoner on a ship bound for Rome. The ship stopped briefly on the island of Crete, but remained too long in a port called "the Fair Havens." Fearing the dangerous winter storms, they attempted to sail up the coast to the safer harbor at Phoenix. However, they were soon caught up in a gale and the ship was driven out of control across the Mediterranean Sea.

God had revealed to Paul that they would go through such a storm if they left at that particular time. However, the centurion paid more attention to the recommendation of the ship's captain and owner to set sail than he did to Paul's warning of impending danger.

In the midst of raging seas and unable to bring the ship to land, they decided to weather out the storm. For fourteen days the storm raged. Finally, in the early morning light, they sighted an island in the distance. In their attempt to land, the ship ran aground and broke into pieces with the violence of the waves. By a miracle of God, none of the two hundred and seventy-six men, soldiers, and prisoners who were aboard died. They had endured both the storm and ultimate tragedy because of the mercy of the unfailing God. As Paul had testified to them during the dark, uncertain hours of the storm, God had spared all of their lives. With some swimming and others clinging to the floating boards from the broken ship, they washed safely up on the shore of the island of Malta, and there spent the winter before proceeding on their way to Rome the next spring.

This miracle clearly demonstrates how many of our troubles come totally unsolicited and how others are the result of our own doing. In this case, the sailors brought trouble on themselves because they were not willing to listen to the warnings of God through the apostle Paul.

HOW TO GET INTO TROUBLE

People get into trouble for different reasons. Some invite it, others are the victims of someone else's wrongdoing, and still others are the victims of circumstances. The sailors found themselves in their predicament for very specific reasons.

First, they followed the wrong advice. Instead of listening to Paul, the centurion followed the advice of the captain and owner of the ship. The resulting disaster could have caused them all to perish.

One of the most tragic mistakes we make in life is following the wrong advice. Everywhere we turn, it seems there is someone offering a wrong choice. Ours is a society of self-appointed experts. We are bombarded by bad advice by friends, neighbors, relatives, television, and even total strangers. It is important to be cautious, even in regard to seeking advice from other Christians. The ultimate issue for the believer is to ask yourself whether or not the advice you receive is clearly based upon biblical truth.

The evangelist Billy Sunday used to relate a story about a woman who boarded a train with her small child during a heavy snowstorm. Because she had never ridden a train before, she was unsure as to where to get off. So she asked the man who was seated next to her if he knew where the Southside Station was in Jersey City.

"Oh, yes," the man replied. "I have been there many times myself; it is the second stop along this route, and I will be glad to tell you when we reach it."

As the train chugged through the New Jersey countryside, the man began dozing off to sleep. He roused when he felt the train stop once and then start up again. He was soon dozing again when he felt the train stop a second time. Waking up, he informed the woman that they were at the Southside Station. The woman thanked him for his advice, picked up her child and her belongings, and disembarked from the train. After a short while, the train stopped a third time. By now the man was wide awake and was shocked to hear the conductor announce that they were arriving at the Southside Station.

"What do you mean?" the man shouted at the conductor. "I am certain the Southside Station is the second stop of this route, and we have already stopped twice."

"The second time we stopped," the conductor responded, "was at a deserted water tank. The engine was overheating from plowing through the heavy snow, and the engineer wanted to see if there was any water left in the tank to cool it down."

"Oh, no!" screamed the man. "I told that woman with the baby to get off there!"

In desperation, they backed the train down the track, looking for the woman. When they came to the deserted water tower, they found her lying in the snow, with her baby clutched to her breast, both of them already frozen to death.

Unfortunately, there are often serious consequences to taking the wrong advice. How many people have walked away from their marriage because they listened to the wrong advice? How many teenagers have destroyed their lives with alcohol or drugs because they listened to the wrong advice? There are countless millions of people who have shipwrecked their lives because they listened to the wrong advice. Be careful from whom you take advice, and make sure that that advice is based upon the truth.

The second reason the sailors got into trouble was that they followed a foolish majority. The majority of the sailors insisted that they could make the journey safely, but they were wrong. The centurion not only based his decision upon poor advice, but he listened to an ill-informed majority. Whenever we follow the wrong opinions, even if they are in the majority, we will always do the wrong things. That is not to say that the majority is always wrong, but the majority is certainly not always right, either.

The basis of Christian decision-making is the Word of God and not the opinion of the majority. Even the majority of Christians may be wrong about a particular issue. We must learn to decide everything in life based upon what the Bible itself clearly teaches.

When Moses was leading the children of Israel in the wilderness, there came a time when the majority of them were convinced that he had made a terrible mistake. They were ready to turn around and go back. Their rebellion was so serious that the majority of them died in the wilderness! Because the majority was wrong, they never achieved the Promised Land.

It is often said that God plus one equals a majority. In reality, God Himself is the only majority we need. Once we are following Him, we need not worry about what the crowd is saying or when they are going in the wrong direction.

Their third mistake was that they depended on a human perspective. The Bible tells us that the sailors decided to embark for the safer harbor of Phoenix when "the south wind blew softly." From their human vantage point, the sky was clear, the winds seemed favorable, and the seas were calm. Sailing seemed to be the logical thing to do. But Paul understood that the time to set sail had passed and that it would only be a matter of time until the weather changed. The sailors discovered just how misleading their human perspective could be.

Satan can also distort and blind our perception. He can literally blind our eyes and twist our minds to the truth. We can actually come to the point where we are unwilling to see the potential destruction which lies ahead, in spite of all the warnings that God may send into our lives.

The real decisions of life don't depend upon our insignificant human perspective at all. They depend upon God's greater perspective. The bottom line is God's opinion, not ours.

The Bible tells us that when God forgives our sin, He actually forgets it. That means that He removes it from His own conscious dealings with us and treats us as though the wrong had never happened. But he leaves the seed of memory in us. So while we know that we have been forgiven, we still remember the impact and consequences of that sin in our life. Allowing us to remember is His way of warning us against future sin. Therefore, even if we have already suffered the consequences of sinful and wrong decisions, we do not have to spend the rest of our lives doing the wrong things as a result of those decisions. There is a way out of the storm if we will take it. It takes courage and confidence in God's process of dealing with our lives, but the results are wonderful indeed.

HOW TO GET OUT OF TROUBLE

As we read the story of Paul's shipwreck, we can certainly understand how the sailors got themselves into such a mess. But how were they to get out of this mess? The storm was raging, the lightning flashing, and the thunder roared as that little ship was tossed all over the tumultuous sea. Even when they finally spotted land and tried to drop anchor, they were driven onto the rocks and the ship was destroyed. In spite of that, as we know, all of them were saved alive.

It was when the sailors had given up hope and were considering abandoning ship that Paul gave them God's reassurance that they would all be spared. By this time, they were finally willing to listen to God's message through Paul. And once they landed safely on the Island of Malta, they were rescued by the local people, and Paul undoubtedly had a captive audience for the next several weeks.

If you have reached a point in your life where you are ready to give up hope and abandon ship as well, remember this: No matter how hopeless your situation may seem to be, God has not given up on you. You may not see any way out of the darkness, but there is a way. You may not understand the solution to your difficulties, but there is a solution. If God could bring Paul and a band of ungodly sailors safely through the storm, He can bring you through your storms as well. Whatever you do—you *must* endure. Here are some suggestions to help you through your storms.

1. Recognize God's Presence in Your Problems.

Just as God was with the apostle Paul and stood beside him in his most desperate moments on that ship, so

He will be with you as well. The Lord has promised that He will be with us until the end of this age. While friends and family may fail you, He will always stand beside you to hold you up in your hour of need. He has promised to be with you and never forsake you. In your moments of difficulties, you must cling to that promise and never relinquish the confident assurance that God will see you through this situation.

2. Trust God's Purposes Despite Your Problems.

When all seemed lost for Paul and the others, God reassured him that he would stand before Caesar and proclaim the gospel of Jesus Christ. God was reminding Paul that in spite of the apparent danger and imminent disaster, He was still in control of his life and destiny. This allowed Paul to stand there with confidence even as the wind was blowing against him and the rain was beating down upon him. He knew in the depth of his soul that God was on his side!

When the storms of life are blowing against us, we must remember that God has a purpose through all our problems. There are no accidents in the life of the believer. Because God lives within us, His purposes are always being accomplished through us. Now I realize that it is easier to say this than it is to live it, but the truth of this principle is just as certain as anything to which we could ever anchor our lives. When all seems dark and hopeless, remember God is still at work, and His purposes are still being accomplished in and through you regardless of circumstances.

3. Claim God's Faithfulness.

God has promised to be with us and see us through this life on to the next. That is a promise on which we can build our lives. Paul's confidence surpassed everyone's on that ship because he knew that he could trust the promises of God. Heaven and earth may pass away, but the Word of God will abide forever. Paul was willing to live his life in accordance with that truth.

The greatest lesson that we can ever learn in our spiritual journey here on earth is to trust what God has said. If we can trust God to forgive our sins, save us from hell, and offer us heaven, we can certainly trust Him with our daily problems!

The promises of God are as solid as a rock. They are the certain ground upon which you can anchor your soul. When the winds and storms of adversity come, that anchor will hold firm because it is grounded in God Himself. As you rest yourself upon His strength and sufficiency, you can remain calm and courageous in the face of whatever comes your way. Hold your head up high, face your storm, and let God produce the miracle of endurance within your heart.

. . . he that endureth to the end shall be saved.

—Jesus Christ, Matthew 10:22

13

MEETING YOUR
GREATEST NEED

■ ■ ■

The Miracle of Provision

Luke 5:1-6

Luke 5:1–6

1   And it came to pass, that, as the people pressed upon him to hear the word of God, he stood by the lake of Gennesaret,

2   And saw two ships standing by the lake: but the fishermen were gone out of them, and were washing their nets.

3   And he entered into one of the ships, which was Simon's, and prayed him that he would thrust out a little from the land. And he sat down, and taught the people out of the ship.

4   Now when he had left speaking, he said unto Simon, Launch out into the deep, and let down your nets for a draught.

5   And Simon answering said unto him, Master, we have toiled all the night, and have taken nothing: nevertheless at thy word I will let down the net.

6   And when they had this done, they inclosed a great multitude of fishes: and their net brake.

God has always been in the business of meeting people's needs. Just when we need it most, His provision is more than enough to meet life's greatest demands. Consider, for example, the miracle of provision found in Luke 5:1–6.

Peter and his fellow fishermen had fished all night and come home empty handed. When Jesus arrived in their village the next morning, He requested the use of Peter's boat as a platform from which to teach. After His message, He asked that Peter once again take the boat out fishing. This must have been a little frustrating for Peter. There is nothing more exasperating to a fisherman than to fish all night and come home empty handed. And on top of that, now he was being asked to go out again!

Peter had undoubtedly tried his very best and had cast out his net in the usual manner, but had failed in every instance. Perhaps you can identify with his struggle. You may not be a fisherman, but you may have attempted another task desperately and failed to achieve it. You may have failed in business or failed in a marriage, or failed with your children. It really doesn't matter at what we have failed, failure still hurts just the same.

Whatever Peter may have thought of the Master's request, he, nevertheless, responded to it immediately.

He gathered the nets, launched out into the lake, and let them down at Jesus' command. The result of this simple act of obedience was that Peter caught more fish at that one time than he had in his entire lifetime. In fact, his nets were so filled with fish that they began to tear and he had to call to another boat to help him haul them in—and even then both boats were on the verge of sinking!

What made the difference? The answer is—Jesus Christ! As soon as Jesus stepped into Peter's boat, the entire scene changed dramatically. To really discover God's provision for your needs, you must begin by getting Jesus into your boat. By that I mean, you must get Him into your life. Once Jesus entered into Peter's life, He so transformed it that Peter was never the same person again. Our spiritual walk must begin with a personal encounter with Jesus Christ as Savior and Lord. There are many terms by which we explain that process of new birth. Our Lord Himself called it being "born again" in John 3. Other passages in the Bible refer to being saved from sin and its dreadful consequences. Others use the term "being converted to Christ." However you explain it or label it, the end result is still the same. When Christ enters one's life, He changes it forever.

I once had the privilege of discussing the "born again" experience with President George Bush. It was in the winter of 1986 when a Congressman invited me to attend a private meeting with the then-Vice-President at a hotel near our church.

"Of course, you know what I'll want to ask him?" I said.

"Certainly I do," he replied, "and that's one of the reasons we want you to meet with him."

So at the time agreed upon I went to the hotel and was ushered into a meeting room for an informal time with Mr. Bush. Writer Doug Wead, who was there with us, later wrote about our conversation in the June 1986 issue of *Christian Herald* magazine. Here is a short excerpt.

> The Atlanta hotel suite grew quiet as the discussion branched away from the agenda. Now the conversation moved beyond issues to personal experience.
>
> The Southern Baptist decided to go ahead and pop the question. "Tell us," he said, "have you been born again?"
>
> George Bush showed no outward sign of fluster. "Yes, I believe in Jesus," he replied, "and I've accepted Him as my personal Savior. There have been moments," he continued, leaning back in his chair, "like being shot down over the Pacific. I was a 20-year-old-kid; the other two men in the plane were dead, and flames all over us. Of course, I cried out to God to save me. I remember floating in that rubber raft in the middle of the ocean . . . and yet, a feeling that God was going to help somehow and that I was going to live.
>
> "So yes, I've had some life-changing experiences that have left me with a profound sense of faith in God. Really that's where the commitment shows. Those are the times when a person reaches deep down inside himself and comes to grips with the question of why God put you here and what does it all mean, anyway?"

I listened attentively as President Bush continued talking about the change his experience with Christ had made in his life, how he was not the same after that moment. And that is my point—salvation changes one's life!

I'm not talking about simply joining a church, walking down an aisle, getting baptized, or making some kind of public profession. All of these are certainly good, and even necessary, but going through them as a routine will not bring new life to a person's heart. Only Christ can transform us on the inside so that the difference is seen on the outside.

Perhaps you have been considering becoming a genuinely committed Christian for some time. Or perhaps God has spoken to you for the first time about this matter. Here are some basic steps to follow to know for certain that God has made provisions for your spiritual needs.

ACKNOWLEDGE YOUR SINFUL NATURE

The Bible tells us that sin is a universal problem of mankind. "All have sinned, and come short of the glory of God," the Scriptures state in Romans 3:23. That means that every person, rich or poor, black or white, educated or uneducated, has fallen under the stain of sin. Each one of us needs a Savior who can forgive that sin and cleanse our hearts.

It is the work of the Holy Spirit to convict us of that fact. As He enables us to see how short we have fallen of the righteous standards of God, we will be overwhelmed by the realization that we need forgiveness. The truth is that we are all in need of the grace of God. As long as we think that we can make it to heaven on our own, we will never come to the place where we realize we need a Savior.

The Bible tells us that Jesus came into the world to save sinners. If the apostle Paul, one of the greatest Christians who ever lived, could call himself "the chief of sinners," how much more do you and I need to face the reality of sin in our lives? Being a sinner does not mean that you have committed every sin known to man, nor does it necessarily mean that you have committed the worst of sins. It simply means that you were born with the nature and capacity for sin within you, and you, like everyone else, need God's help in overcoming it. One day we all will stand before Christ in judgment. For those who know Him as Savior, it will be a judgment of reward and rejoicing, but for those who have rejected Him, they will stand before their own judgment of condemnation.

The greatest thing that matters in life is how you stand with God. Marilyn Monroe was the ultimate goddess of Hollywood, but when she died, all that mattered was how it was with Marilyn and God. Elvis Presley was "the King of Rock and Roll." But when Elvis died, all that mattered was how Elvis was with God. John F. Kennedy was young, wealthy, educated, and powerful. But when a rifle was fired on the streets of Dallas, all that mattered was how John Kennedy stood with God. Someone wrote these lines that say it so well:

When the great plants of our cities,
Have turned out their last finished work,
When the merchants have sold their last yard of silk,
And dismissed the last tired clerk,
When the banks have raked in the last dollar,
And paid out their last dividend,
And the Judge of the earth says, "Closed for the night,"
And asks for the balance, What Then?

When the actor has played the last drama,
And the mimic has made the last pun,
When the billboard has displayed the last picture,
When the crowds seeking pleasure have vanished,
And gone out in darkness again,
And the trumpet of ages is sounded,
And we stand before Him, What Then?

When the choir has sung the last anthem,
When the preacher has prayed the last prayer,
When the people have heard the last sermon,
And the sound has died out in the air,
When the Bible lies closed on the pulpit,
And the pews are all empty of men,
And the trumpet of ages is sounded,
And we stand there before Him, What Then?

Author Unknown

COME TO REPENTANCE

It is not enough to simply understand that you are a sinner unless you are willing to do something about it. We can understand all about the seriousness, and even the consequences, of sin and never really repent of it. Repentance is mentioned 969 times in the Bible. From Genesis to Revelation, the Scriptures declare that we must repent. The Old Testament prophets preached repentance. The apostle Paul preached repentance. Even the book of Revelation calls us to repent.

What does it mean to repent? First of all, repentance is confessing that sin exists in your life. It involves an admission of sin. For those coming to Christ for the first time, repentance generally means their admission to the fact that they are sinners.

Second, repentance involves a change of attitude about sin. The term *repentance* in the Greek New Testament comes from the word *metanoia,* which means a "change of mind." When we change our minds about something, we inevitably experience a change of direction as well. If you were engaged to be married to someone and then changed your mind about them, the end result would be that you would break off the engagement and no longer continue toward a commitment of marriage. The same is true in relation to genuine repentance. Once we acknowledge our sins and change our attitudes about them, we will stop defending them and excusing them. Those who have never repented of their sins spend most of their lives trying to excuse those sins or justify their existence in their lives.

Third, repentance results in rejecting sin and going in the opposite direction. The Old Testament word in Hebrew for repentance was *shub,* which literally means "to turn around." Once we acknowledge our sin and begin to see it as God sees it, we will begin to develop a hatred for that sin. The alcoholic or prostitute knows that he or she is a sinner. But that does not mean that they are willing to repent and do something about it. Once we see sin as repulsive and rebellion against God, we will want to turn away from it.

It is this third aspect of repentance that is often confusing to people. There are those who say if you turn away from sin on your own efforts, you are trusting only in your good works to get you into heaven. Then there are those who have promoted a kind of easy-believism salvation, which implies that one may believe in Christ without repenting of sin. Both extremes are equally dangerous. We cannot turn our backs and go in to the opposite direction by our own self efforts. But as the Spirit of God convicts us of sin and begins to work the process of regeneration in our hearts, He will turn us in the opposite direction. That is why the Bible places so much emphasis on the changed life of the believer as the ultimate evidence of true salvation. Therefore, the Bible says, "If any man be in Christ, he is a new creature: old things are passed away; behold, and all things are become new" (2 Corinthians 5:17).

Salvation comes as a result of faith in the finished work of Christ on the cross. We cannot add to that work and to our salvation in any way. We cannot make ourselves turn away from sin apart from the spiritual empowerment of God Himself working in our lives. However, the truth which is taught in the New Testament is that the true believer in Christ, who has committed himself to the Savior, will experience a life-changing turnaround as a result of the grace of God at work in his life. It is this change which becomes the evidence that God has indeed transformed us from the kingdom of darkness to the kingdom of His dear Son.

CONFESS YOUR FAITH IN JESUS CHRIST

The Bible places a great deal of emphasis on the importance of public confession. The Scripture says, "If thou shalt confess with thy mouth the Lord Jesus, and shalt believe in thine heart that God hath raised him from the dead, thou shalt be saved" (Romans 10:9). This passage in particular places a great deal of emphasis on the importance of public and verbal profession of faith. The Bible also tells us that it is through the mouth that the heart of man really speaks. Therefore, if your mouth is any indication of your heart, it will readily acknowledge your commitment to Christ. Jesus also made the point that if we were unwilling to confess Him before men, He would be unwilling to confess us before His Father.

Everything that Jesus did for us was done publicly. When Christ was born, God hung a star in the heavens to publicly announce His birth. When He died on the cross, Jesus suffered a public execution in which even one of his captors said, "Surely this man was the Son of God!"

What's unfortunate is that many today who claim to be Christians take the attitude that perhaps it would be best not to tell anybody at work, or school, or in the neighborhood that they have committed their lives to Christ. Some actually accept the false idea that it is better to become a kind of secret agent for God, lest they scare anyone away. Those people are already away from God and are likely to stay away unless we speak up and share with them the wonderful joys of personal fellowship with God.

Public profession of faith inevitably means a willingness to acknowledge Jesus Christ as one's Savior and to openly confess Him before men. This includes following Him in believer's baptism as a public testimony of your death to sin and resurrection to a new life in Christ. It also includes a willingness to publicly and personally acknowledge Him verbally as you give testimony to your faith in Christ. Finally, public profession involves your association with a local body of believers who share that same faith and commitment to Christ. These actions of personal profession will not produce your salvation, but they will certainly give evidence as to its reality!

SUBMIT TO JESUS AS LORD

Jesus is frequently referred to in the Gospels as *Lord* or *Master*. Once we have accepted Christ as our Savior by faith, we must submit to His authority and lordship over every detail of our life. In other words, receiving Jesus as Savior *and Lord* is paramount to receiving the whole person of Christ to meet the needs that we have as sinners.

There are many people who profess Christ as their Savior but are unwilling to acknowledge His authority as Lord over their lives. Peter could have easily taken the attitude that Jesus was a carpenter and could not match Peter's expertise as a fisherman. Instead, Peter recognized Jesus' spiritual authority and responded with faith that resulted in obedience to that authority and in an incredible miracle that otherwise might not have happened.

It is virtually impossible to separate faith from the results which it produces. The Bible makes it clear that works do not save us, for salvation is based upon faith alone. But the Bible also teaches that genuine faith results in spiritual works which are an evidence of true salvation. When Jesus told Peter to launch out into the deep water and let down the nets, He was testing his faith in Him. Peter could have said, "Lord, I really believe in you, but I don't intend to do as you say." Such a profession of faith would have seemed ridiculous in light of the Savior's command.

Some of us are what could easily be called shallow-water Christians. We are willing to follow Christ as long as it involves wading around in knee-high water. But when it comes to launching out into the deep water and really trusting Him, such professing Christians are reluctant to put their faith into action. People who make a half-hearted commitment to Christ are the kind who attend irregularly, give spasmodically and complain incessantly! When the deep waters of life come rolling over them, they usually go under!

Jesus said that in order to be His disciples, we must be willing to deny ourselves, take up the cross and follow Him. To deny literally means to "disown." It actually means to put yourself to death. Such self-denial is central if we are to experience His complete power and blessing. There is no place for merely playing religion or playing church in such a life of total commitment to Christ. When we make that kind of total surrender to Christ, He will become Lord of our business, our family, our lives, and everything that we own.

It may sound ridiculous at first to allow Christ that kind of control over your life. But it is only when we are willing to do the ridiculous that God is willing to do the miraculous! And there is nothing ridiculous about the powerful and complete salvation which Christ provides for us. As we learn to obey Him step by step in our lives, we begin to progress in our spiritual walk with God. The Bible calls this process sanctification. That term literally means that God is in the process of making us into holy people. Our relationship to Christ marks us as unique people whose lives have been touched by the grace of God. He has made every provision for our every need and we shall never again lack spiritually in this life or the life to come!

Perhaps you have never experienced the forgiveness of sin. Perhaps you would like to pray to receive Christ as your Savior. Here is a simple prayer that you might pray to God to receive His dear Son.

Dear God, I ask you to forgive my sin. I believe that your Son, Jesus, died on the cross that I might be forgiven, and rose again on the third day that I might have eternal life. Therefore, I trust His finished work by faith and receive Him into my heart as Savior and my Lord. Amen.

Once you have put your faith in Jesus Christ, repented of your sins, confessed Him as your Lord, and begun to live in obedience to His will, you can expect the miraculous power of God to start its work in your life. Then, not only will you have been part of a miracle—God will have made a miracle out of you.